FAMILY GARDEN

FAMILY

GARDEN

A practical guide to creating
a fun and safe family garden

LUCY PEEL

HarperCollins*Publishers*

First published in 1999 by HarperCollins*Publishers*

99 01 03 02 00
2 4 6 8 9 7 5 3 1

Text © Lucy Peel 1999

A CIP catalogue for this book is available from the British Library

ISBN 000 4140699

Editorial: Sue Hook and Antonia Maxwell
Picture research: Joanne Beardwell
Index: Sue Bosanko

Colour reproduction by Colourscan
Printed and bound by Rotolito, Italy

The HarperCollins website address is:

www.**fire**and**water**.com

CONTENTS

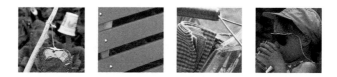

planning a family garden

It is amazing how often all a family's energy – creative and physical – is reserved for the home, while the garden is left as an afterthought. This is all the more surprising when you consider the large amount of time spent in the garden and how it can enhance quality of life and even health. Thinking purely in monetary terms, your property is your single greatest asset and to neglect the one thing – the garden – that can add so much value to your home is sheer folly.

Before embarking on any work in the home or garden set aside time to work out exactly what you want and draw up detailed lists and plans. No time spent in planning is ever wasted. In fact it can save a great deal of money, effort and frustration.

▶starting from scratch

Below
An undeveloped garden is a wonderful opportunity to plan your garden according to your family's needs.

Many young families are attracted to new housing estates. They offer afford-able, brand new houses with builders' guarantees, banishing maintenance worries for a good few years.

They also offer the prospect of other young families to befriend. as well as conveniently placed facilities such as playgrounds. medical centres and shops.

Planners and builders of new estates often concentrate all their attention on the houses rather than their gardens. These tend to be left as small bare rectangles of either mud or grass. Although such spaces may look uninspiring they offer a wonderful oppor tunity to create something entirely suited to your family's needs and personalities. Think of them as a blank canvas.

The first thing to do is to examine the soil. Once the hastily laid turf is peeled back. it usually reveals a rather unappealing mixture of rubble with the thinnest sprinkling of top-soil. So if your home is less than five years old. the first thing to do. before you rush out and buy lots of plants. is to set about improving the soil. This may involve buying and work-ing in more topsoil. You should incorporate as much organic matter as possible to make the soil nutritious and ready to take plants.

Next look at the surroundings of the garden. There may be a busy road which you would like to screen off. or the garden may be overlooked by neighbours' windows. making privacy a priority. There may also be vast expanses of bare wall or fence which could be improved with a clothing of climbers or painted in an attractive colour.

▶ working with what you have

Below
A circular patio softens the appearance of a square or rectangular garden. Containers also add interest.

If you have moved into an old house there will probably be an established garden. This may have been beautifully kept or be a jungle, but either way there are bound to be things you wish to change or adapt.

Consider the shape of the garden. If it is very square you may wish to soften it by creating curved borders with flowing planting. Awkward triangular or long narrow plots can also be transformed through design – narrow sites by adding a diagonal feature (be it a flower bed, steps or a path) and triangular by creating a circular shape, for example.

Once your basic framework is in place you will be ready to think of adding the plants which provide structures, colour, perfume, flair and flounce – the more transient stars of the garden.

As soon as you move in, walk around the garden and do a safety check. Remove any obvious hazards, such as poisonous plants (see Chapter 7), barbed or rusty wire and crumbling walls, and cover ponds until you have time to consider safety measures. Mend or remove loose paving stones and trim back any dangerous branches and shrubs.

Do not be too hasty in removing established shrubs. You may not find a particular plant appealing, but it may provide a useful framework while other plants are becoming established. It is surprising how much better a shrub can look after pruning and with new planting around it. After all, if it does not grow on you, you can always take it out later.

Left
Think about the amount of time you have to spend in the garden. A garden with shaped lawns will require more work than one with straight edges, although you may think it worth the extra effort.

Above

Think carefully before you remove any large plants and structures such as trees and walls. Spend time getting to know your garden before making any large decisions.

Delay starting major work until you have been in the garden for a full year. You need to see a complete cycle of seasons to appreciate fully just what is in your garden, and how all its elements work together.

A delay will also give you the chance to watch how your children play in the garden. You may be surprised at the features that attract them. For example, an overgrown hedge which you had earmarked to be grubbed up may prove to be the perfect site for a den. You may have planned to buy them a climbing frame, or metal-framed swing, only to discover that they are getting such enormous enjoyment from climbing the trees

that a swing from a sturdy branch, rope ladders, commando-style netting and even a tree house would be much more appreciated.

Throughout the year make notes about the elements of the garden that give you most pleasure and those that annoy you. In practice you may find that the drying area is too far from the house, that the outdoor lighting is insufficient, or that the position of external taps is impractical. On the other hand you may discover that a flower border which seemed out of place is ideally positioned for maximum/minimum sunlight, frost risk and perfect drainage. And what a wonderful excuse not to do any work in your first year!

▶assessing your family's needs

Every family is different, with its own unique mix of personalities and requirements. So before you start any work on a garden have a good long think about your family, their likes and dislikes. Take time to examine your everyday domestic routines and your leisure time.

Are your home and garden always overflowing with your children and their friends? Do you enjoy entertaining? Are you quite an active person who cannot sit still for a minute, or are you always looking for the opportunity to relax with the papers and a cup of tea in a quiet corner?

Get everyone to make their own wish list. You may get some highly impractical suggestions, but they will give you an idea of how each member of the family views the garden and how they would like to use it. You need to complete your list of family requirements before you can start planning their position in the garden.

Don't feel obliged to think in traditional terms: if nobody is bothered about a lawn, a vegetable patch or a flower bed, then don't have one. You can always change your garden later when your family's requirements change.

▶ practicalities

Divide your list into headings. First come practicalities, the mundane domestic needs of everyday life. These may be tedious to think about, but getting these details right will make the difference between an easy-to-run house and garden, and one full of little irritations – daily reminders that you could have done better if only you had given the project a bit more thought.

Above and below
Remember to plan storage space in your garden. Toys, equipment and furniture all need to live somewhere when not in use.

storage

Every family needs storage space – for toys, bicycles, garden furniture and equipment. This should be of an adequate size for your requirements, easily accessible and securely lockable. Sometimes you can use part of a garage or have an area in your home that can be used, but if not a shed is the most sensible solution. Work out how much space a shed will take up, and work this into your plan. Sheds are available in all sizes including small lean-to designs, so there is bound to be one to suit your garden and budget.

refuse

Space for bins is important. They should not be too far from the kitchen, yet you will also want easy access to the front gate for refuse collection. The area should be lit and you should also consider whether you need to build an enclosure as protection against vermin and pets. You may also want to think about ways to disguise them, such as fencing, so allow space for this too.

drying facilities

You will need easy, all-weather access from your washing machine to your clothes line. This should not be too far away from the house, in case you need to make a mad rescue dash if it starts to rain. Think about what sort of drying facility you prefer. There is a wide choice of dryers, including rotary lines (choose those set in sockets so they can be removed) and retractable lines. Consider safety, allow plenty of room for washing to flap without getting tangled in nearby plants, and remember that whatever you choose will need space and will affect your view of the garden.

Above

Careful planning of your front garden will make life much easier. Allow enough space for cars and bicycles, and a covered walkway is useful in British weather. Use low-maintenance plants and consider not having a lawn for an easy life.

kitchen garden

This should be close to the kitchen, otherwise visiting it will become a chore rather than a pleasure. You will need easy access to water in the form of a strand pipe, hose extension, or water butt, as well as to the compost heap and greenhouse.

car parking

Now that most families have at least one car, if not two, a driveway, car-port, garage and hard-standing for parking must be considered. Many homes will already have garaging and parking space so their position will be fixed. However their relationship to the rest of the garden can be altered by planting. For example, the walls of an ugly garage or car-port can be made to disappear behind a wall of shrubs. Climbers can be planted to scramble up the walls and cascade over the roof, and the edges of the driveway can be softened by spreading plants.

lighting

You will need different sorts of lighting for different purposes (see Chapter 5). Convenience and safety are important, but remember that well-planned lighting can also transform a terrace and highlight unusual garden features.

maintenance

How much time do you have to spend on gardening? This is a very important question. Be realistic, as there is absolutely no point in persuading yourself that you can easily look after huge borders of herbaceous plants, when in fact you would be hard-pressed to prune a few shrubs and cut the grass.

▶leisure time

Onto the interesting part – planning your leisure time in the garden. Start by listing the fun things you plan to do, or dream of doing, in the garden.

eating outside

Everyone enjoys eating outside, so building or adapting a terrace should be top of the leisure list. At the same time you could consider a built-in barbecue. A permanent barbecue can also double as an outdoor fireplace which will prolong your time spent outdoors.

playing

For children playing takes precedence over everything else, so most children's wish lists will include every play structure, piece of equipment or toy imaginable. Decide what is most suitable for your children, as well as what will fit in the garden, bearing in mind that, as they grow, you may want to adapt or modify their play space.

Right
You may choose to include a patio area for eating outside or for somewhere to sit and read the newspapers.

Left
Water is popular with many people, and depending on the age of your children, you may want to add a water feature. A shallow pond lined with pebbles is a more attractive option than one lined with plastic, and it needn't cost a fortune.

lounging

For pure relaxation all that is needed is a comfortable chair, or hammock, and some peace and quiet. If you have space, incorporate features, a summerhouse or an arbour.

water features

Water safety is the main concern when planning a water feature. If you have young children, a pond may be out of the question, but there are several safe options to consider (see Chapter 3).

attracting wildlife

If your garden is full of insect, animal and bird life it will not only be a more interesting place for your family, but a healthier, more balanced environment in which pests are gobbled up rather than killed by chemicals, and where plants thrive helped along by pollinating insects. So leave some wild corners and plant plenty of insect-attracting and berry-bearing shrubs that are attractive to insects and birds alike.

decorative features

These can elevate a garden out of the ordinary. Pergolas and arbours wreathed in plants convey a soft romantic touch, while an urn, statue or other ornamental feature can add a wonderful element of surprise.

child's garden

You could plan to put aside a piece of the garden for your children to call their own (see Chapter 7) or you could plant trees to commemorate special events, such as births and anniversaries. Children will quickly come to love their tree, and you can keep a record of the tree and your child's progress with yearly photographs and a height chart for both tree and child.

be extravagant!

Family gardens are the ideal place for you to indulge your imagination with light-hearted, playful features that reflect the personality of your family. Include a few oddities such as a sundial clock, or sink bricks with the hours painted on them into the ground in a circle and position them so that when the child stands in the centre of the circle their shadow falls across the correct hour.

You could include something to appeal to adults and older children, such as a giant chess and draughts board made with dark and light coloured pavers. Hopscotch and noughts and crosses also lend themselves to this idea. Most gardens are too small for a full-size croquet lawn, but a modified version is possible. You could also construct a sanded rectangle for boules or *pétanque*.

Above
This incredible sundial is sited on a small lawn of thyme surrounded by clusters of pebbles. It is a stunning piece of sculpture and would be a talking point in any garden.

making a plan

Sketch a rough scaled plan of the house and garden on a large sheet of graph paper. Start with the house and any outbuildings, and mark downstairs windows and doors. Add boundaries, such as hedges, fences and walls, and all trees, shrubs and beds that you want to keep. Terraces and paved areas, steps, paths and ponds are all vital, as are changes in ground level. Include the canopies of overhanging trees and mark in stars for good views or features. Indicate north and the direction of prevailing wind and the path the sun takes over the garden during the day. Label very shady, very sunny, very wet or very dry areas.

Once you have completed your rough sketch, measure your garden and all the permanent features and draw up a clean, precise plan. This will help you make logical decisions such as where to site hard landscaping features. Your terrace should not be sited where it gets a raging gale, but where it receives the gentle warmth of the evening sun. Your plan will help you satisfy both these requirements, as you will able to tell at a glance the direction of the prevailing wind and where the sun shines at different times of day. The plan will also help you avoid such disasters as erecting the children's swing then finding out that their feet get tangled up in the branches of the apple tree as soon as they gain some height, or setting up compost bins at the end of a path that is just too narrow for the wheelbarrow to get down.

All this may sound a bit daunting, but it is actually very straightforward and is essential in getting to know your garden. It is an important exercise that helps you clarify ideas, work out which features and plants will suit the garden, and how to make it a truly user-friendly garden.

Always consider the garden in relation to the style, proportions and scale of the house. There should be a smooth transition between the two – each must flow into the other. Think of the garden as an extension to the house, an extra room. Go around the house looking out of windows. Views into the garden are extremely important.

Allow the landscape, shape of the site and surrounding areas to guide you. A strongly urban landscape has as much to offer as rolling fields. Look for natural assets which can be highlighted or borrowed, such as a view – maybe this could be opened up and made more of? Beautiful mature trees and

Above
Curved lawns and abundant planting make this a stunning garden. It will, however, require daily maintenance to keep its shape.

Right
Careful design will enable you to make the most of your available space.

Above

Trees provide shade and privacy. They hardly need any looking after, and are a great addition to a family garden.

attractive neighbouring buildings or a beautiful wall can also be valuable features, so make the most of them.

Some features of the site cannot be altered without great expense, for example if the ground is naturally very hilly. So make these level changes work for you by creating an intriguing series of terraces linked by winding paths or steps. Each level can be quite different in character to the last and the children can have their very own terrace for playhouses, swings and climbing frames. Such gardens have a wonderful feeling of movement and space to them, with each terrace offering new delights to entice you to explore further.

While some drawbacks may not be totally overcome, they can be alleviated in many ways. Shade can be reduced by judicious pruning, eyesores, such as oil tanks, can be

disguised or screened, and even a strong prevailing wind can be partially tamed by planting a barrier hedge to dissipate it.

The most basic rule of all is keep the initial design strong and simple. You can always add to it later.

When deciding what to plant, don't confine your thoughts to colour, perfume and size. There is so much more which is important – such as shape, texture, movement and sound. However, it is a very good idea to restrict the varieties of plants and colours. A border planted with bold clumps of flowers, maybe in a single colour, looks much more striking than one containing a wide variety of plants in different colours dotted here and there. Remember to plan your groups so that the smallest are at the front.

Trees are always a welcome addition, providing vertical interest, character, shade and a place to play or sit. Many people are put off planting trees by the thought that they may take a long time to grow, or because they plan to move on after a few years. But even a young tree will add enormous interest to your garden, and with many species it is amazing how much growth can be put on in just three or four years.

Choose your tree carefully, avoiding thirsty or strong-growers such as willows (*Salix*) and poplars (*Populus*). These have a wide-ranging root system which may damage house foundations or hard surfaces such as paths and patios. Instead look for trees which offer year-round interest in terms of shape, bark, blossom, berries, delicate new spring growth and spectacular autumn colours. Flowering crab apples (*Malus*) are lovely, as are varieties of maple (*Acer*), rowan (*Sorbus*) and birch (*Betula*).

Try to picture how your garden will look as the seasons progress. You need to sustain interest throughout the year, so note when individual plants will look their best for flower, fruit or foliage and site them so that they can be enjoyed from your main vantage

points. Obviously your soil type may rule out certain plants, so if you are desperate to include them plant them up in containers.

Don't forget safety aspects (see Chapter 7) and avoid plants that are poisonous, have irritating sap or are dangerously spiky.

Finally, remember that children do not stay little forever, and as they grow they will change their ways of using the garden. Instead of wanting a climbing frame, they may eventually prefer a secluded scented bower where they can chat or read in privacy.

So be patient. If you have always yearned for a pond, and are not able to have one while the children are very young, they will soon be old enough for water to be safe. If you adore delicate flowers and enormous herbaceous beds, there will be plenty of time to get these established once the children demand less of your time and have stopped kicking footballs about.

Above
A large flowerbed in the centre of a lawn can look great, but will require maintenance and may suffer after several games of football!

Right
If you have space, consider dividing your garden into an area for children to play, and a quieter corner where you can escape from them.

surfaces and boundaries

Once you have decided your plan for the garden, the next stage is to think about surfaces and boundaries. Before you think about soft landscaping, such as a lawn and flower beds, decide if you are happy with your hard landscape, such as the fences, walls, steps, terraces, decks and pergolas. You need to get the hard landscaping right before you can move onto the gardening, as it is the all-important framework within which the beauty of trees, shrubs and flowers will be contained.

▶boundaries

Boundaries represent more than just a marking of territory; they are important for privacy and security. They keep unwelcome humans and animals out as well as children in and they should also be designed to improve the look of the garden.

Top
An arch can divide the garden, marking a change in usage.

Above
Using fences and hedges within the garden as a divider provides privacy and creates an illusion of space.

When deciding on a design and materials bear in mind the period and style of your house, as well as the materials it is built with. The boundary should be in keeping with the house and blend with the rest of your design.

hedges

A living boundary in the form of a well-tended hedge is not only an asset to a house but to the local wildlife. And nothing beats a hedge as a wind-break and as a baffle to deaden noise.

The most suitable style of boundary hedge will depend on the design and surroundings of the house. For example, a very formal clipped hedge would not suit a country cottage surrounded by fields, while a mixed country hedge would look rather strange outside a white stucco town house.

Other things to consider when planting a hedge are height and spread and its speed of growth – this will determine how often you need to cut it. Choose hedging plants which will do well in your soil. Look around at neighbouring gardens to see what looks healthy and happy as there is no point in trying to grow a lime-lover in acid soil. Also consider whether the plants will get enough light as they are growing and whether the ground is too dry. All these factors will determine how quickly the hedge grows and how dense it will be when mature.

As far as wildlife is concerned, a good mixture of native evergreen and deciduous hedging shrubs will be the most popular for nesting birds, food and shelter. However many people prefer an evergreen hedge for year-round privacy. This kind of hedge makes a strong shape which noticeably defines the boundary. If security is a worry, whether it be keeping unwanted visitors out or children in, a few prickly, spiky shrubs, such as holly, pyracantha and berberis, make very effective barriers.

Good alternatives to evergreens are deciduous shrubs which retain their leaves in winter. Beech (*Fagus sylvatica*) and hornbeam (*Carpinus betulus*) are excellent examples. In the autumn their leaves turn a lovely warm golden-brown but do not blow away, hanging on until the new buds appear in spring.

The main disadvantages of hedges are the time they take to establish and their maintenance. Hedges are also wider than a wall or fence so need more space. They are, however, worth the effort and if you are worried about the need for a temporary

Above
Ivy and a stone mask add interest to this beautiful stone wall.

Right
A hedge reduces the space in this small town garden, but it provides privacy and greenery for very little effort. The topiary balls continue the theme.

Below
A plain concrete wall has been transformed using shells stuck on with more concrete.

barrier you can put up a cheap fence and plant the hedge in front of it. When the hedge has reached the desired size, you can remove the fence.

walls

Nothing beats the look of a well-built brick or stone wall, especially one that has weathered naturally. Its warm rich look makes it a thing of beauty in its own right, even before it is clothed in climbers.

Walls can be built of brick, stone, concrete, or even large boulders piled on top of each other without mortar to make a dry stone wall. They make a sympathetic backdrop for climbers, and if south-facing, hold the sun's warmth, creating an ideal position for fruit trees, such as figs and pears.

However, a properly constructed wall, even a very low one, is very expensive, as the cost of labour must be added to that of materials. Another disadvantage is the wind factor, as solid walls create an area of wind turbulence which can harm plants.

fences

A fence provides an instant solution to the boundary problem. There are numerous different types, many very cheap, and they are usually very easy to erect as most types come in prefabricated panels.

Among the cheaper types of fencing are larch or pine overlap, or basket weave. If you want something a bit more unusual look for woven willow or hazel wattle hurdles. These are more expensive as they are handmade by craftspeople, and will not last more than five or six years, but they are

Above
Add interest to a standard overlap fence with containers, climbing plants and a decorative trellis.

Below
A wicker fence creates a relaxed country look, and is a good backdrop to a climbing rose.

extremely attractive, look wonderfully rustic, and work especially well as a stopgap while a hedge establishes.

These more open fences also work well as wind breaks, as they allow enough wind to filter through to diminish its ferocity. To achieve the same effect with a solid fence, attach trellis to the top and clothe with a mass of climbers.

Open fences, such as ranch and picket fences have a great deal of charm but do not provide much privacy, shelter or security, so use sparingly.

If you have spare soil on site from excavations for ponds or level changes try something completely different and erect a Cornish fence. This looks spectacular yet is very easy to erect. It consists of a wall of earth about 60cm/2ft wide by 90cm/3ft high contained between two hazel wattle

hurdles. The hurdles are lined with marine ply for strength and durability. Once it is all in place the earth is firmed in and planted up.

railings

Cast iron railings, often set on top of low walls, were very popular in the eighteenth and nineteenth centuries, especially in the fashionable areas of cities.

In Europe and Australia many railings were removed during the second world war, to be melted down to make armaments, so it is quite difficult to find reclaimed railings. However, it is possible to buy modern cast iron railings. They are not as heavy as the originals but are just as ornamental and will add a welcome, classic, finishing touch to a formal town house.

▶dividers within the garden

Hedges, walls and fences also have a role within the garden. They can be used to define and protect a particular area, such as a kitchen garden, or to create interest, variety and structure in your garden layout.

An open garden can be made more intimate by a series of hedges planted to create different garden rooms. corridors and walkways. By dividing a garden in this way it can be made to seem much more extensive. and if it is planned properly with clearly defined paths. visitors will find themselves drawn to walk around the garden. exploring each twist and turn.

Informal low-growing hedges. such as lavender and potentilla. work extremely well as internal dividers where the density of the hedge is not a major consideration.

Trellis. especially the decorative types with concave or convex tops and elegant dividing posts topped with finials. looks extremely smart when used to divide different areas of a garden. It is good-looking enough to use on its own and once clothed with jasmine or passion flower looks even more spectacular.

gates

Gates are a feature in their own right. They can be plain. functional and simple. or they can be decorative focal points. Whether you prefer ornate or plain gates they should match both the house and the boundary in style. if they are not to appear completely out of place. A modern. cast iron gate looks totally wrong set in a beautiful. old. stone wall. just as an elaborate Victorian gate does not work in a contemporary setting.

Besides self-closing child-proof catches it is well worth fitting rising buttress hinges on any external gates. The advantage of these is that they always swing shut. so children will be less able to wander and burglars will not be alerted to an apparently empty house.

▶paths and driveways

Below
Crazy paving looks attractive in a country garden, especially if made from stone or natural-colour pavers.

Paths and driveways are vital elements in the design process, as they not only link the house with the outside world, but, in the case of paths, different areas within the garden.

The shape you decide upon for your paths and driveways will have as much an effect on the impression they create as the materials they are surfaced with. A straight front path and driveway will create a feeling of formality and purpose and are usually best suited to small front gardens. Curves and undulating shapes look more natural and create a sense of movement and freedom. tempting visitors to explore. especially if your front garden is large. with the house set well back.

The overall shape of your plot and where the house stands within it will determine whether you choose straight lines or curves. A straight driveway and path may seem a little too ordered. but work extremely well with either a very modern house or. at the opposite end of the scale. an old. grand house. A curved. or even circular driveway. with a curved path to the front entrance. will look at one with most country houses.

While practicality is obviously important. it is also vital to choose surface materials which look good and are in keeping with the style of the house. garden and boundaries. All these considerations apply to paths around and through the back garden. A garden design is like a jigsaw in which no one element can ever be viewed in isolation and each part must slot together to make the whole picture.

driveways

Most visitors approach the house via the driveway. so it is vital to give this area thought when planning. After all. first impressions are important and so it is not enough just to choose the most functional shape and surface material.

As the driveway adjoins the house take the colour of the house as a guide to the ideal colour of the drive. A slightly deeper shade of the same colour looks best. If you try to match colour and shade exactly the result may look rather boring.

Above
Covering the driveway with climbing plants softens the look of the area and looks welcoming.

Right
It is a good idea to add a path in an area that you use frequently.

paths

Paths can serve several functions in a garden. If you have a path leading to your front door instead of a driveway, think about the impression it creates (see also the section on driveways). Paths also exist to link or divide different parts of the garden.

Obviously the quickest route between any two points is a straight line, but a straight path will not necessarily do your garden justice. If a path is allowed to meander, with plenty of curves and little surprises along the way, such as a shady arbour with a bench to sit on, or an interesting focal point to draw the walker on, it will help transform your garden into a place of magic and mystery. Be aware though, that people may be tempted to take shortcuts, which could damage your lawn.

Use planting to create paths with different atmospheres. For example, trees and shrubs can be planted alongside the paths to create a tunnel effect. To make this even more dramatic plan the tunnel so that it emerges into a bright, open area of the garden. The contrast will be delightful.

You can make an entirely different tunnel effect by erecting a pergola or a series of arches, planted with fragrant climbers. Enhance the romantic effect by placing an urn mounted on a plinth, a piece of sculpture, or an attractive container at the end as a focal point.

There are also numerous tricks you can employ which fool the eye into thinking the path or garden is longer than it is or which change the shape of the plot.

A particularly effective illusion is to lay the path so that it gradually gets narrower and narrower. This will make it seem longer than it actually is. Or design a mysterious path which disappears behind a dense shrub or hedge. You may have nothing behind this other than a garden shed, but it will create the impression that there is a whole new area of the garden, just out of sight.

If your garden is noticeably oblong or square, you can make use of a path to alter the visual perception of the shape. Simply lay the path so that it runs in a semicircle around the edge of the garden, creating a circular area of grass or hard surface in the centre. This draws attention away from the hard boundary lines.

▶surface materials

Paths and driveways must be practical as well as attractive. Firstly they must be wide enough for comfort and secondly they must be constructed of materials which look good, fit in with the design of the house and garden, are hardwearing and safe.

Below
Bricks are inexpensive and easy to use. As they are so small, you can make a patio area any shape you like.

To decide which materials work best for your needs and within your design, look at the garden as a whole, examine how the different elements hang together visually and consider the needs of your family. For example, a gravel drive always looks extremely smart and suits any style of house, but might your children like to cycle on the drive and paths and do you need to push a buggy along them? If the answer to either of the last two questions is yes, then it may be better to abandon the idea of gravel.

Safety must also be considered. A slippery surface is a recipe for cuts and even broken bones, so must be avoided at all costs. York stone slabs and brick surfaces can be particularly slippery in wet or icy conditions.

The choice of surfaces for driveways and paths is enormous and are far more attractive than the old standbys of concrete and tarmac. There are paving slabs, tiles, bricks and cobbles, as well as precast setts. Look for local materials, as these are more likely to blend in with existing elements in your garden. Be sure to check with your supplier that your choice can take the weight of a car.

Paving materials will look very different depending upon how they are laid. Small units such as setts and bricks, are quite busy, and square paving slabs can look totally different if laid point on, resulting in a diamond as opposed to grid pattern. Combinations of two materials of different size and texture, such as brickwork and paving slabs, can work very well together.

However, whichever material you decide upon, the end result will only be as good as the foundations it is laid upon. Like any building or gardening job preparation is all-important. Be sure to lay your driveway and paths on a properly consolidated base of hard-core with, if necessary, sand on top. Build in a very slight camber to allow water to run off away from the house. If you neglect this, water will gather, eventually damaging the surface and posing a danger in freezing weather. Avoid trees within 5m/16ft of paths or driveways if possible, as the shade may make the surfaces slippery and the movement of roots may lead to unevenness or subsidence.

concrete

The main advantage of concrete is that it is cheap and easy to lay. It is also hard-wearing and does not require much maintenance. Concrete is an extremely flexible material and can be bought as slabs, poured into moulds to make shapes or laid direct on to a hardcore base and then finished either by smoothing or by imprinting to create any number of patterns. It can also be colour tinted numerous shades.

The rather harsh look of a large expanse of concrete can be lessened considerably by combining it with large pebbles, brickwork or cobbles. These provide a visual distraction and break up the monotony. If you already have a concrete drive or path and want to smarten it up, then dig up sections, breaking up the concrete with a pickaxe or drill, fill with concrete then inset any of the above materials. Keep your design simple and, if in any doubt of your abilities, call in a professional.

stone and paving slabs

Original, stone slabs always look extremely handsome, with their feeling of solidity and patina of age. Reclamation yards usually have good stocks, but they are expensive. A cheaper but equally attractive alternative is reconstituted stone slabs. These are man-made from precast concrete and aggregates. There is a huge range and they are so realistic it is virtually impossible to distinguish them from stone. Like the real

Left
This path is made by squashing coloured stones and pebbles into wet concrete. You could do this for a whole path or just in a few places to add interest.

Left
Alternating colours can make ordinary pavers look more interesting.

thing they also age, improving with time and exposure to the elements until they become pleasantly mellow.

cobbles and precast setts

Cobbles and setts look wonderfully natural and are extremely hard-wearing, although, cobbles are not very comfortable to walk on for long distances. Original cobbles can be difficult to obtain and laying them is a job for a professional. If it is not done expertly individual cobbles can work their way loose and be difficult to reset.

Another option which looks just as good is precast setts. This is a relatively new process which uses variously coloured concrete or clay in a mould to produce a surface indistinguishable from the real thing. The end result is very tough, and the wide choice of tints allows you to find just the right shade to suit your house and its surroundings.

Above
This path has been made by pressing stone slabs into the soil and allowing the grass to grow around them.

tiles, brickwork and pavers

The patterning in bricks and pavers comes not from the material itself but from the pattern of laying. Among the most common patterns are herringbone, stretcher bond and basket weave. Tiled paths work very well in an urban setting, particularly on the path leading to the front door, where they look suitably formal. They are probably not suitable elsewhere in the garden where they are liable to crack and become dangerously slippery with heavy use and exposure to planting. Slipperiness can also be a problem with bricks and some pavers, although a thorough clean with a high pressure jet or a scrub with a stiff brush and soapy water will help keep the problem in check. Avoid special moss and algae treatments as they are unnecessarily harsh and will eventually take the surface off the tiles or bricks.

When choosing tiles and bricks check that they are frost-proof, otherwise they will soon start to flake and crumble. Pavers are very tough, being designed to withstand the weather and wear from cars and feet.

Clay and concrete tiles are available in every pattern and colour imaginable, and while the choice of colour for bricks and pavers is slightly more limited, it should be possible to find some to match your house without much difficulty.

gravel and chippings

Gravel and chippings are both stone products. They are relatively cheap and can transform the look of a garden, giving it instant style. They come in a variety of colours, which makes them excellent for matching with masonry or paint and washed or pea shingle or chippings will also lighten up a dark area — a huge advantage if the front of your house faces north.

Do have shingle or chippings laid properly. Just tipping out a lorry-load, then spreading it around with a rake won't do. It may look good for a short time but rainwater will soon start to gather and in no time at all there will be weeds sprouting everywhere.

If you lay gravel on top of another surface, such as concrete or tarmac, first spray the whole area with hot bitumen, sprinkle a single layer of shingle or chippings, then roll. Once it has dried you can add more loose material on top to the finished depth recommended by the manufacturers. This ensures that you will never reveal the subsurface even when a car turns and moves the top layer. Alternatively it is possible to buy a self-binding gravel.

The downsides of shingle or chippings is that they are difficult to cycle or push a buggy or wheel barrow over, both can cause nasty cuts if fallen upon and chippings have a tendency to spread into the flower beds and house. If you are concerned about children hurting themselves then choose either washed or pea shingle, as these have no sharp edges.

The other problem is that local cats may decide to use your gravel as a giant litter tray. They can be discouraged from small areas with strong-smelling substances such as crushed mothballs or cat pepper.

▶steps
and edges

Above
Large pieces of slate
make great steps.

Below
Railway sleepers and
gravel make unusual
and stylish steps.

Many gardens have different levels to be connected, even if only from the patio to the lawn. Ramps may be necessary if the garden is used by the elderly or wheelchair-bound, but for most families steps are the best and most practical solution. They can be extremely beautiful in construction and materials, with incidentals, such as pots or plants, completing the picture and making them a decorative feature in their own right.

It is important to get the correct proportion of rise (the height of each step), depth and width of the step. Aim for shallow steps, with a minimum rise of 10cm/4in, and a minimum depth of the treads of 30cm/12 in. Make sure the steps are even and solid when finished, with the slightest tilt to ensure water drains off easily.

The material you choose for your steps should depend on the style of the house and garden and should tie in with other materials used in the construction of the garden. They can be built from any of the materials listed for paths and driveways, plus a few additional options, such as railway sleepers and preservative-treated logs.

Where steps lead down from a terrace they should be constructed of the same materials in order to look at one with it. Proportion is an important consideration. For example a narrow flight of steps leading up to a broad terrace would look odd when a wide sweeping flight of steps is ideal.

Above
Wood blocks are ideal for edging areas of loose materials such as bark chips.

Left
Containers placed on steps add interest.

design

When siting your steps it is important to consider their primary purpose. Are they simply fulfilling a practical need, for example, connecting the patio to the lawn, or are they to play a more decorative role? Whatever you decide influences their position. If they are mainly decorative, you may decide to follow the natural contours of the land so that they twist and turn. If, however, they are purely functional their position is more restricted.

The geography of the site also has a bearing on the most suitable shape for a flight of steps. In a steep, craggy, seaside setting the steps may have to wind around rocky outcrops, while straight, wide, shallow steps can easily be accommodated in a garden set in gentle rolling countryside.

formal or informal?

The style of your house and garden should also determine the style of your steps. In a formal garden, elegant, curved, stone or brick steps, flanked by uniform pots filled with clipped box or bay look very stylish.

Certain materials lend themselves to particular settings. Stone paving slabs are completely appropriate in a formal garden, while informal, or contemporary gardens allow for much more experimentation. Old railway sleepers, for example, are sturdy and cheap and make excellent steps, especially if teamed with gravel as an infill. Preservative-treated logs are also suitable and look perfect in a wild or woodland setting. Wood becomes slippery when wet, but a sheet of chicken wire securely nailed over the logs or sleeper will solve this problem.

edgings

To finish off and retain steps and paths an edging is needed. It may be nothing more than planks of wood laid on their sides or you can choose from a huge range of purpose-made edgings which make the job easier and look smart.

For a purely functional area that is tucked away in a corner, such as a kitchen garden, plastic or aluminium strips, or concrete edging are efficient but unattractive. A more pleasing alternative is to use bricks placed diagonally on end. These are decorative, easy to lay and look equally at home in rambling cottage gardens and more formal settings. For a more natural look particularly suited to woodland gardens, use edgings of treated logs or large stones. Shells can fulfil the same function in seaside gardens, but can be damaged easily.

To add an historical feel to your garden you might choose drawn wire edging or, if you need something more substantial, rope-top, fluted or scalloped Victorian-style edging tiles. These more expensive edging materials are made in either terracotta or concrete and are available with little posts and finials for the corners.

Laid securely and with care all these edgings will enhance the look of your garden by helping to define different areas preventing gravel, earth and stones from spreading where they are not wanted and making mowing infinitely easier.

Above
This path is made from bark chips and is edged with willow canes and tufts of oregano. Bark chippings are great for children, as they provide a soft landing.

▶ patios, verandahs, decks and balconies

No garden is complete without some-where to sit, preferably a space large enough to take a table and chairs for alfresco meals. If you place a table and chairs on grass, it cuts down the time you can use them, as the grass will be dewy in the morning, and will quickly get damp and cold in the evening. Chair and table legs sink into damp earth, so you will have to move them every time you mow, and in time, the grass beneath them will become muddy and compacted. The obvious solution is to build a hard-surfaced area which can be used all year round.

Below
The design of this garden emphasises the different areas and their uses by different surfaces. The dining area is patio and there is a grass play area for children.

In cities, where space is at a premium and gardens small, paving over the whole garden to create a patio (originally meaning a paved, walled garden) may be the answer. However if your garden is larger, you may be able to set part of it aside to build a separate patio or deck.

patio

A patio is usually the hard-surfaced area immediately adjacent to the house, though you could site it elsewhere. You can integrate the patio with the rest of the garden by using the same materials to surface it as are used elsewhere on driveways or paths. Whatever you use should tie in with the materials of the house, especially as your patio will be used primarily as an outdoor room. Additional continuity can be achieved through harmonious planting.

Whatever you build must be large enough to accommodate a table and chairs and for people to move around behind the chairs if desired. You may also want to include enough space for containers and possibly one or two garden loungers and an umbrella. You could also consider space for a sand pit or barbecue.

Be sure to include some herbs in your planting plan. They not only look attractive, but scent the air and are useful in the kitchen. Most herbs love hot, dry conditions and cope well with neglect, so are fine in containers, even if you forget to water them occasionally. Fragrant climbers planted to scramble up the walls of the house will help prevent the patio looking stark, and a simple water feature will add extra ambience (see Chapter 3).

decks

Long popular in Australia and the US, decks have only recently become fashionable in the UK. They are built of wood and can be erected anywhere in the garden or as a patio immediately adjacent to the house, providing a link between indoors and out.

Wood is a lovely, warm material which, if properly treated, wears well. It requires minimal maintenance, but can be slippery when wet if not treated with a non-slip coating. Splinters can also be a problem so use timber that is planed smooth for decked surfaces.

Decks offer versatility and are therefore particularly useful in steep, sloping gardens, or where there are a large number of trees, as it is very easy to build the deck around them.

As timber is such a natural material, plan the surrounding planting informally, so creating the impression that the deck has somehow grown out of the garden. Bamboos work well, as do plants with large leaves and exotic foliage, such as varieties of *Rheum palmatum*, *Fatsia japonica* and giant grasses.

verandahs

These are part of the structure of the house and should therefore be treated in a slightly different way from patios, terraces and decks, even though these form a bridge between house and garden.

A verandah is usually roofed, so it makes wonderful all-weather play area for children. It should be broad and shady, a place of retreat from the blazing summer sun and an all-purpose outdoors room where families can take meals, play, chat and even do homework. You could prolong your use of this extra room by investing in an outdoor heater.

Lush planting, in pots or beds alongside the verandah, will increase a feeling of coolness, and a few pots of flowers which release their fragrance at night, such as lilies (*Lilium longiflorum*) or tobacco plants (*Nicotiana alata*), will encourage guests to linger.

balconies

Balconies are a special attraction in urban settings with small gardens. Carefully planned they provide a peaceful haven from the noise and smells of the streets below but it is vital to take safety factors into consideration. Before planning any balcony check with a qualified surveyor that it is structurally sound with a damp proof surface and capable of taking the weight of containers filled with wet soil, plus any furniture.

As surface space is limited, vertical planting is especially valuable. Trellis arches secured to the house walls provide an easy purchase for twining climbers and look decorative in winter when the foliage has died back.

Plant colourful clematis and perfumed white jasmine (*Jasminum polyphyllium*) and fill containers with scented flowers and shrubs. As balconies are elevated they tend to be exposed to the elements, so look for plants which cope well with drought and winds. Shrubs such as *daphne* and *skimmia* will be quite happy, as will *pelargonium*, *nemesia* and *helichrysum*. Pots of clipped lavender and rosemary look smart and provide delicious fragrance.

Left
Decking can also be used as a pathway through a garden.

Right
This family have used decking across the whole garden, doing away with the need for a lawn. This cuts down on maintenance, but do bear in mind that decking can be very slippery when wet, so this might not be suitable for young children or the elderly.

▶ grass and alternatives

Hard surfaces make for hard landings, and as children spend so much time falling over – whether from a rough tackle at football, a mis-timed jump over the skipping rope or nothing more than tripping over their own feet – a child-friendly surface is called for.

Below
Looking after a lawn can be hard work but it is ideal for children to play on. Choose a hard-wearing strain of grass if you don't want your lawn to turn into a mud bath.

grass

The most obvious surface is grass. It looks good, is a pleasure to sit on and smells delicious when just cut.

Most families enjoy an area of grass to sit or play on, and the key to keeping a family lawn looking good is to choose a suitable grass mixture for your needs. Those including resilient rye grass are ideal for a hard-wearing lawn. Don't mow too short, but set the blades higher than you would for a luxury lawn so that the minimum finished length is 2–2.5cm/3/4–1in. This is particularly applicable when there are water shortages as the lawn will look better when slightly longer.

In heavily-used areas, such as that beneath a swing or climbing frame, lay rubber mesh with black rubber matting tiles on top. These are held in place with specially designed pins. The mesh spreads the load and ensures the tiles do not damage the turf and, as the grass grows up through the mesh and tiles, it hides them completely. The joy of this system is that it both protects the grass, and allows you can to mow whenever you please.

alternatives

If you live in a very wet climate it may be better to choose an alternative surface, because grass takes quite a while to dry after rain and can all too easily deteriorate into a permanently muddy quagmire.

natural

Much-used areas, such as the ground beneath a swing, can become so com-

pressed that it is as hard as concrete. Here a few bags of chipped bark, which is available from any garden centre, should be laid as a mulch. It instantly creates a surface which looks totally in keeping with its surroundings and provides a very soft landing.

Sand is also a good surface under swings and climbing frames. However it is best avoided if you have pets, as they may decide to use it as a giant litter tray.

man-made

Over the past few years a number of man-made crash surfaces, previously only seen in municipal play grounds, have appeared on the market. These consist mainly of treated cork or porous rubber matting and tiles, which come in every colour of the

rainbow. They are excellent, safe surfaces with built-in bounce and are weatherproof and tough enough to cope with extremely hard wear. The downside is that they are relatively expensive and many should be laid by a professional qualified contractor. It does, however, last for years, and when the children have outgrown the area, it could then be used as an alternative area for outdoor dining.

Artificial turf has been around for many years and, although it is also fairly expensive, it is a good all-weather surface which has proved itself very durable. It is easy to maintain, needing only the occasional hose-down, and it is simple to lay. It provides a gentle landing, and will withstand much more wear-and-tear then real grass.

Above

Bark chippings have been used in playgrounds for years and they are now available in garden centres. When your children have outgrown their play area, use the chips on your flower beds to keep weeds at bay.

furniture and equipment

Furniture must do more than look good and suit the style of your house and garden. It must be comfortable, strong and able to withstand daily family life. Few families have an elastic budget, and although you may prefer a quality piece that will last for years, it may be more practical to buy more temporary items. Do, however, spend as much as you can manage on sturdy, safe, well-constructed furniture.

For practical purposes it is important to consider maintenance and storage when choosing furniture. Does it stack or fold, and if so, have you somewhere to store it, or is it robust enough to be left exposed to the elements all year round? This chapter also looks at other features and equipment you may like to include in your garden, including water features and sheds.

▶chairs and tables

Above
Folding chairs are easily stored. This one has a hole in the back so it can be hung up out of the way.

Below
Solid wooden furniture is timeless and looks great in a garden. It will also last for years.

Visually, chairs and benches may be decorative enough to act as focal points, drawing the eye towards a particularly attractive spot. They should tempt you to rest, contemplate and enjoy the beauty of the garden. It may be that a warm, sheltered spot is ideal or, if you prefer, a refreshingly cool, shady corner.

wood

Solid wooden furniture is very natural, very sturdy and will last a very long time. There are many handsome designs available, both traditional and modern, in a wide variety of grades and finishes of timber.

Hard woods, if left to weather naturally, will gradually develop a beautiful silvery patina. However, should you wish to maintain its original colour, an annual rub down with oil is all that is needed. Soft woods, preferably pressure-treated with preservative and finished with a preservative stain will last well. Coloured woodstains will not give long-term protection as they do not penetrate the wood deeply enough.

A practical choice for families with young children is a wooden picnic table with built-in benches. These work well in informal gardens and are extremely safe, especially if you have young children who are prone to tipping over chairs. There are scaled-down versions available which look are ideal placed outside a playhouse or in a children's garden.

plastic

Plastic chairs are unbeatable for comfort, as they are moulded to the shape of the body. They are tough and able to cope with any weather. They need nothing more than the occasional wipe down and they are

stackable, thus reducing storage headaches. Yet while they may be practical they are not often very attractive. White soon looks grubby and scuffed, so choose a dark colour, such as green, and dress it up with smart green and white stripy seat cushions and a matching tablecloth to improve its appearance. Most plastic tables can be collapsed for winter and those that cannot be folded up usually come with protective covers. A table with a hole in the middle for a parasol is particularly useful.

Above, top
Deck chairs are favourites in the garden. They also look good indoors, especially if you have a wooden floor.

Above
Iron furniture is expensive, but very hard-wearing. Add cushions from your indoor dining chairs or living room to make it more comfortable.

canvas

Canvas directors' chairs are extremely smart, very comfortable, and are just the right height for dining and fold up, so are easily stored. However, as material does not cope well with getting wet and can be hard to clean, it is best to avoid very pale colours. Directors' chairs look equally good teamed with solid wood, metal or plastic tables.

metal

In recent years wrought and cast iron garden furniture has undergone a tremendous revival and now there are many wonderfully delicate, curly, or dramatic gothic designs on the market. Lightweight alternatives are cast aluminium or wirework furniture, which share the good looks of wrought and cast iron – although both will rust. Metal furniture is very elegant and,

dependent on its style, suits formal period and minimalist town gardens alike. It can be left outside all year as a permanent garden feature, and being so ornamental makes a strong, moveable focal point. In general, however, metal is colder and less comfortable than wood.

stone, slate and marble

Garden furniture made from these materials is grand enough to attract the eye, yet definitely not portable, so consider its position carefully. It is possible to buy a ready-made table, but these are expensive and it may be more fun and much cheaper to put one together from different pieces found in reclamation yards, for example, slips and hearths from old fireplaces. Some quarries and stonemasons also sell direct to the public. Stone weathers beautifully, growing silver or orange lichen in sunny spots and velvety moss in shady ones. A coat of natural yoghurt will help speed up this process.

rustic seats and tables

Whether roughly hewn from solid logs, or made of twiggy larch poles, rustic seats and tables look home-made and eccentric. It is this quality, and the knowledge that they are one-offs which makes them so attractive. Like wrought and cast iron furniture a well-made piece makes an excellent focal point in a garden.

wickerwork

For a 1920s or '30s look, wickerwork, cane and Lloyd Loom furniture is worth seeking out. Very comfortable and lightweight, these pieces are only really suitable for fine weather or the conservatory, but look just as good indoors or out so can be stored in the house during winter. It can still be found in very cheaply in junk shops and although it may not be possible to find complete sets, you can achieve a personalised and stylish look by mixing and matching.

Above
A wooden seat wrapped around a tree looks very stylish and blends in well with garden surroundings. You can buy kits that will fit around any tree.

café chairs

French café chairs, made of metal and wooden slats, are extremely light and fold flat. They are best kept for dining rather than lounging as they are somewhat small and flimsy – qualities which make them the perfect choice for a balcony or small terrace. For a truly continental feel, look for matching, round, metal tables.

benches

Perfect for a sun-soaked terrace or secluded corner, there are endless varieties of bench available, from curvy metal and plain teak, to stately Lutyens-style. Old-fashioned barrow benches are perfect if you want to enjoy several corners of your garden, as they can be rolled along, following, or even avoiding, the sun. Stone benches retain the heat so are very pleasant to sit on, although if you linger too long they may start to feel painfully hard.

Try to find a place in your garden where you can build an informal seat, such as in the retaining wall of a raised flower bed. Don't be afraid to experiment. For example, build a marine ply or brick frame, fill it three quarters full of rubble, finish the top quarter with topsoil, and then plant chamomile (*Chamaemelum nobile*) to create a living seat. Chamomile does not mind being sat on and will release the most delicious fragrance. Extremely popular in England in Elizabethan times, such seats were said to aid relaxation. Also exploit any natural features your garden may have, such as a grassy bank and if you need to cut down a tree, leave the stump as a little table for the children to picnic around.

Any garden with trees should have a tree seat. These can be smart cast iron or, delightfully rustic, made of wood. It is possible to buy kits, which are very easy to assemble and do not require any sawing or sanding. Simply varnish, stain or paint and you have a beautiful and practical feature which everyone can enjoy.

For a morning coffee or relaxing evening drink a swing seat is irresistible. Simple swing seats can be made from a plank of wood and attached to a secure beam, branch or the roof of a verandah by strong chains or ropes. More elaborate, freestanding swings are also available, with metal frames, comfortable padded cushions and waterproof canvas canopies.

recliners

The cheerful striped canvas of deck chairs has long conjured up images of outings to the seaside. Unfortunately deck chairs are also associated with jokes about people getting hopelessly muddled as they try to put them up, falling through worn canvas and struggling to get out of them. Yet modern deck chairs have come a long way since then, and while it is still possible to buy the traditional style, there are alternatives available which are simple to erect and have arm rests for comfort and to help you get up. In short they have become fashionable classics, and as they fold flat are an excellent choice if space is tight.

Metal, tube-framed loungers with foam-filled, removable, padded cushions are inexpensive and widely available. They are

Right
Traditional wood and canvas parasols are worth the extra investment because they are sturdy and will withstand years of use by a family. They also tend to be larger than metal-framed parasols, which mean that more people will benefit from their shade.

very comfortable and are easily adjustable to recline at different angles, from upright to flat. The other great bonus is that they fold flat and are extremely light.

The kings of recliners, steamer chairs get their name from the fact that they were first used on cruise liners, but their smart, sleek and timeless design looks just as at home in a family garden. They are extremely sturdy, being made usually of solid teak with removable cushions – so are an excellent long-term investment. The main drawback is that they are expensive.

The ultimate portable recliner is the hammock. No grown-up can resist the lure of a hammock on a hot summer's day. Once the preserve of gardens with trees, it is now possible to buy free-standing hammocks, or those with a v-shaped frame holding one end while the other is attached to a tree. Canvas or woven material hammocks are preferable to string mesh, which can be quite uncomfortable unless made of pure cotton.

parasols and canopies

Some sort of parasol or canopy is essential to protect your family from the sun. There are beautiful, traditional wood and canvas parasols now available. Besides being reassuringly heavy they tend to be larger than the metal and cloth parasols and look luxurious as well as decorative. They are slightly more expensive than metal-framed parasols, but add such class to a garden that they are well worth the extra money.

There are various gazebo-style canopies that are particularly useful for gardens without natural shade. These canopies are made mainly of water-proof cotton and galvanised steel tubing, so are lightweight and can be easily collapsed for storage. Some are large enough to eat under, while others are just big enough to accommodate a few chairs. Canopies with mesh sides are especially useful, as these can be rolled up to allow cooling breezes to enter, or lowered if insects are a problem.

▶water features

The sound of running water is not only relaxing but extremely refreshing. The play of light on the surface of a pond, the flash of colour and sparkle as sunlight catches a splash of spray from a fountain, all add an inimitable quality which can lift a garden from being merely pleasant to being spectacular.

The Moors in Spain understood these qualities. In the Alhambra garden in Granada, there are numerous pools, fountains and rills and the air is filled with the musical sound of water. Even if you don't have such grand plans, you can still use water to great effect.

ponds, pools and rills

Still pools, ponds and rills make peaceful places to sit beside and contemplate. The reflection of the sky, clouds and trees in the water is hypnotic and tranquil and the gentle rustle of reeds or grasses makes a pleasantly soothing sound.

Parents of very young children are understandably nervous of water and although a pond or rill can be made safe with metals grids it may be wiser to think in terms of an alternative water feature such as a pebble pool or wall-mounted trickle fountain. However, for families with older children a pond, pool or rill should not be dangerous and will provide hours of entertainment.

Below
This millstone fountain set on a bed of cobbles is very safe for children as the water runs off the stone so never collects to any depth. It is also strong enough to survive lots of climbing.

The most suitable type of pond or pool for a family garden is informal, with plants spilling over the edges and a natural looking beach of pebbles. Gently sloping sides will be appreciated as much by wildlife as paddling children (see Chapter 6).

It is possible to buy a pre-formed rigid pool but it is more fun to design your own pool, using heavy-duty butyl or PVC liner. Dig the hole to the depth and shape you desire, remove any sharp debris, lay a thick 5cm/2in layer of sand, spread out and smooth the liner, then fill with water. Next hide the edges of the liner under a mixture of large stones and smaller pebbles, soil and gravel, then plant up.

A pool will soon develop its own ecosystem, with insects, snails and frogs colonising it. When choosing type and number of fish consider their ultimate size and whether they will be able to cope with winter. Your stockist will be able to supply you with this information. Also remember that fish need to eat and that frogspawn is a fish delicacy. So if you want frogs to breed you will have to build a fish-proof enclosure in which the spawn can develop

into tadpoles and subsequently frogs.

Oxygenating water plants are vital to the health of the water, providing the oxygen without which nothing else will survive. However, many water plants are extremely invasive so vigilance is required to keep them under control.

Rills, or straight narrow channels, are particularly suited to formal gardens. A long rill might run along the middle of a paved area with a summerhouse at one end and give pleasure to both grown-ups and children. Adults will appreciate its elegant symmetry and classicism, while children will enjoy the thrill of sailing boats and spotting fish.

miniature pools

Any sort of water-tight container can be made into a freestanding or sunken miniature pool, complete with water plants. Being small such containers are more manageable in terms of safety, as a grid can be fixed just below the surface of the water and the plants threaded through it, hiding it almost completely.

Above
This raised pond edged with logs has a small fountain made from terracotta plant pots. The logs make a nice seat but you will need to watch young children when they are near the pond.

Above
This stylish rill is
connected by small
waterfalls coming
from pieces of slate.

Right
A millstone fountain
would be ideal for a
small garden. Again,
this is a safe water
feature as the water
does not collect to
any depth.

As long as they are frost-proof, old wooden half-barrels, stone troughs, terracotta urns and ceramic Chinese dragon jars all make excellent water features. Filled with irises, glyceria and dwarf water lilies they can look spectacular, and if the container is large, you could even consider adding fish.

fountains

If you want the sound of water but do not want to bother with plants then a free-standing fountain may be the answer. These should not be sited alone on a lawn or terrace, but set amidst a sea of ferns or other foliage where they will look extremely striking. The wide range of designs, from traditional Victorian and Edwardian to contemporary stone and terracotta fountains, means that it is easy to find the right one to suit you and the style of your garden.

Wall fountains are attractive features, which look as good in modern urban gardens as in formal period settings. Mounted on a wall or brick plinth, they mostly consist of an all-in-one unit made up of a decorative mask which spouts water into a bowl. The water is pumped back up to the fountain via a plastic tube by a small unit hidden within the mask.

It is also possible to buy the elements separately and fit them together as you wish. This allows you to alter the distance between the water spout and bowl, which will affect the sound – the further away the bowl is from the spout the louder the sound of the water.

You can choose from a wide range of styles including fish, gargoyle or animal head masks in terracotta, stone, lead or even fibreglass, with the water spout coming out of the mask's mouth. Any sort of proportionately sized container can be used to capture the water. Shallow stone shells, half barrels and pithoi all work well, and for extra safety, fill the container to the top with pebbles. Even 5cm/2in of water depth can be lethal to a small child.

The safest water features of all are bubble fountains. These consist of a container completely filled with large pebbles. Beneath the pebbles is a hidden pump and a reservoir of water, into which a plastic tube is placed. This is fed through the pebbles for water to bubble out. The tiny jet of water should be just strong enough to keep the pebbles glistening wet – a cooling treat for hot, little, bare feet. But do bear in mind that mischievous children may want to pick out all the pebbles and chuck them around the garden.

▶decorative features

Water features are without doubt decorative, yet any garden will also benefit from the addition of a structural feature. A well-placed urn, sculpture, statue or *objet trouvé* will add immeasurably to the character of your garden and a bower, summer-house or grotto always adds a touch of romance.

an old wooden half-barrel or terracotta pot bursting with flowers would look smart and totally in keeping.

You can use containers to create focal points. Grow a brightly coloured shrub in a container then move it as it outgrows its pot to fill an awkward gap in a border. Containers also allow you to grow shrubs or perennials that would not normally take to your soil. Camellias and azaleas, for example, like an acid soil so are normally out of the question in alkaline areas, so mix up an ericaceous compost, pot it up and cheat nature.

Think laterally when choosing containers. The most unexpected articles can look splendid planted up. For example an old butler's sink, tin hip bath or watering can will take on a new lease of life when filled with colourful flowers. By the sea an old holed dinghy packed to bursting with nasturtiums looks colourful and characterful. Chimney pots, especially castellated ones, are eagerly sought after yet are still relatively cheap, and are especially useful as they add height to a grouping of pots.

There are so many terracotta and glazed pots available that as long as they are frost-proof, you can find one suitable for every style of garden. Coloured pots allow you to reflect an overall colour scheme which you may have chosen for hard landscaped structure and planting.

For a more formal or oriental feel seek out ceramic dragon jars, which you could emphasise with colour-coordinated planting. Wooden Versailles tubs are excellent for framing doorways or steps, or you could plant two tall sunflowers to stand to attention beside a bench or doorway.

Group containers of different shapes and sizes together for the most dramatic effects. This not only makes watering easier but reduces evaporation. Placing containers on damp gravel also reduces water loss.

Old lead urns and planters have a lovely soft look and feel to them, but are classified

containers

As previously emphasised, the design of the house and garden should guide all your decisions on style, size, materials and position of all your garden furnishings. After all, nothing looks more pretentious than an unpretentious cottage or modern semi with an enormous grand urn in the middle of the front lawn. The result is pompous and laughable rather than impressive, whereas

Top
This MDF garden bench has had two large holes cut into it so that containers can be inserted.

Above
Group containers together for maximum impact. This way they are also easier to water as you won't need to walk all around the garden with a watering can.

as antiques and therefore extremely expensive. Luckily there are now many faux lead pieces on the market which look exactly like the real thing yet cost a fraction of the price, so no one need be deprived of the pleasure of owning such a classic feature.

Urns and some of the largest terracotta containers and pithoi have enough presence and grace to stand empty. However if you decide this looks a bit stark and you want some plants, keep your choice simple. Less is definitely more when it comes to planting up an urn. Stick to one or two plants and colours. A busy mixture may look good in a tub but will detract from the stateliness of an urn.

For smaller gardens, window boxes, hanging baskets and wall-mounted pots are invaluable. They provide the means to add an extra splash of colour when all the growing space on the ground is full. Hanging baskets should positively groan with their mass of foliage and flowers, tumbling down until the basket is completely obscured. Window boxes look best positioned just below the level of the window, so that you can look down upon the plants without any risk of them blocking out light. Wall pots such as galvanised steel pots look good on their own, even before you add the plants!

what to grow

Besides the obvious flowers and climbers, experiment with herbs, vegetables, fruit, even small trees.

herbs

Herbs grow easily in pots. In fact some herbs, such as mint, are best restrained to prevent their invasive habit. Parsley, sage, oregano, basil and chives will all grow happily in hanging baskets, window boxes and containers. Place a window box on your kitchen sill or fix a 'rise-and-fall' hanging basket to a wall outside, and you will have freshly growing herbs immediately to hand. To flank a doorway or flight of steps a pair of clipped bays will look very stylish.

vegetables

The most commonly grown containerised vegetable is tomatoes, however they also thrive in hanging baskets and window boxes, as will peppers, chillies and miniature aubergines. Lettuces and cabbages are decorative enough to grace any window box and mangetout, runner and French beans planted in a pot and trained to scramble up a wall or wigwam of bamboos will look very pretty. Tripods or wigwams pushed into pots also make excellent supports for squash, courgettes and cucumber. Even potatoes and carrots can be grown in containers.

fruit

Strawberries are often grown in specially-designed terracotta containers with holes in their sides, yet many types of fruit trees will also thrive in large containers. Specially-bred ballerina apple trees take up little space and in spring can be moved to a spot where everyone can enjoy their glorious blossom. Plums also do well in containers and figs actually fruit better if their roots are contained. Miniature orange and lemon trees look delightful on a sunny terrace or balcony, but must be taken indoors at the first hint of frost.

▶large decorative structures

Even a small garden will benefit from some sort of decorative structure, whether it be a tiny summerhouse that doubles in winter as a storage room, or a pretty arch framing an entrance.

Classical statues are generally more suited to grand formal gardens than family gardens, although clever positioning can vastly improve the appearance of a mass-produced statuette. Reconstituted stone or cement lions, for example, given a few coats of natural yoghurt or liquid manure to speed up the ageing process and concealed in the midst of a leafy border can look quite dramatic.

Not many people can stretch to a piece of original sculpture for the garden, but you can elevate found objects, such as an interestingly shaped piece of driftwood, stone or shell, into pieces of art by placing them on a home-made brick or sawn timber plinth, chimney pot or upturned length of clay pipe.

Choose your setting carefully. The intersection of two pathways, the end of a series of arches or a backdrop of a dark dense hedge will show off your chosen object to the full.

Old garden implements, such as a rusted roller or old-fashioned wheel barrow make exceedingly good decorative features. The rule is that nothing must look contrived, however contrived it may actually be.

Sundials are pretty features that children adore. As they follow the changing shadows on the dial they will not only chart the progress of the sun across the sky, but learn to tell the time.

An effective way to liven up a border is to add vertical interest with obelisks made either of trellis or metalwork. It is a relatively simple matter to make an obelisk from four uprights and pieces of trellis, topped with a finial; however metal ones are also available in flat packs, with pieces

Left
Plant a tree or paint a bench to mark a special birthday. There is a wide range of weatherproof paints, in some great colours, available from large DIY stores.

Above
Even a piece of driftwood found on a beach makes an interesting feature in the garden.

Above
Old gardening objects such as this watering can look good tucked into a flower bed. An old roller or a stack of broken pots would also make attractive focal points.

which easily slot together. Train some colourful climbers up your obelisk and you have a smart focal point.

Transform a simple seat into a place of beauty and calm by surrounding it with a bower. Or provide welcome shade from the sun by erecting a beamed wooden arbour over a patio and using it as an attractive support upon which to train scented climbers and vines. Construct a pergola and smother it with roses and honeysuckle and you will not be able to resist wandering through it, breathing in the delicious fragrances.

A piece of topiary is always eye-catching. Experiment with simple shapes, such as balls and domes, before attempting anything more complicated such as a spiral or an animal. It is very easy to clip a pyramid shape with the help of a frame or to create a piece of false topiary. Any dense shrub such as holly, yew, box, *viburnum*, or sweet bay *lonicera* is ideal to work with.

Summerhouses and gazebos are more serious structures, yet need not be ruinously expensive. Carefully placed, painted or colour-stained and clothed with clematis and jasmine, the humblest pre-fabricated building becomes irresistibly romantic.

These are features for all the family to use. For adults a gazebo or summerhouse makes the most perfect spot for relaxing with afternoon tea or an evening drink, and children will treat it as a rather exotic and grand playhouse.

For a truly original feature let your imagination run riot and create a grotto. This is an excellent project for all the family, as even the littlest child can make a contribution to its decoration. Choose your darkest corner and build a rough brick or stone semicircular wall. Fit a wall mask fountain (a gargoyle's head would be ideal) then give the wall a coating of cement and call in the family to dress it up by pressing shells, coloured pebbles and pieces of mosaics into the wet cement. Plant dark green ivy to climb over the grotto and surround it with a selection of ferns.

▶tools and storage

A beautiful garden naturally needs to be maintained and to do this all sorts of equipment is required, from humble spades to high-tech hedge cutters. As when buying plants the key is to buy the best. This may seem extravagant initially, however it will pay in the long run, for good quality tools, if well maintained, will last many years.

Below
A lick of paint can make a boring garden shed a bit more interesting, as can a couple of wall pots.

With electrical equipment, safety is paramount. Thick gloves, goggles and boots must be worn, an RCD (Residual Current Device) fitted, and the tools should never be used in damp conditions.

Always follow instructions carefully as to the correct way of holding a tool with the lead looped out of the way. If hedge cutting, or trimming trees, use a stable ladder and make sure someone holds it steady. Never lean too far forward, tempting though it may be to reach that last untrimmed area.

hedge trimmers
There are three types of hedge trimmers: electrical, petrol-driven and rechargeable. Electrical hedge trimmers are the cheapest, are light and give good results, however the cord can be a hindrance. Petrol-driven hedge trimmers produce excellent results and it is a pleasure not to have to worry about trailing cables. However they are heavy, noisy and expensive. Rechargeable trimmers are the safest, but have limited power and are tedious to recharge.

chainsaws
Never attempt to use a chainsaw, whether petrol-driven or electric, without basic safety training. Like hedge trimmers, electric chainsaws are quieter and lighter than petrol-driven machines, but do not have as much power, so are not suitable for very large gardens with numerous trees.

mowers
Any garden with grass requires a mower and the size and type you choose will depend on the area that needs cutting. There is an enormous choice, with a mower available for every type of lawn.

Hover mowers are perfect for small lawns. They will also, along with strimmers, make light work of awkward corners, slopes and edges, so for big gardens, are wonderful additions to the lawn task force.

Rotary mowers are the best tool for tack-

Right
This small gazebo
structure makes an
attractive shed, but
take care to keep
chemicals and sharp
tools locked away
from children.

ling long grass and rough ground, but do
not give the fine, sharp cut of cylinder
mowers. These produce either a utility cut
or quality trim suitable for a luxury lawn
and are best for achieving a striped finish.

If you have a really large lawned area
then a petrol-driven ride-on mower will
take hours off your time spent grass cutting. Although if you have any sharp bends
or corners you will need a trimmer or hover
mower to finish off.

shredders, shearers and weeders

Every garden produces its share of prunings which are too woody for the compost
bin. A shredder reduces this material,
saving you the effort and waste of burning
it and helping to improve your compost.

Powered shearers and weeders have the
advantage over manual tools in that they
take a great deal of the effort out of tedious
back-breaking jobs. However weeders are

not as accurate and thorough as their manual equivalent, and shearers are only really
suitable for small lawns.

automatic watering systems

Any busy gardener (and that must include
anyone with a family) will find an automatic watering system the most wonderful
time-saver. There are a number of different
systems from which to choose and they can
be particularly good for balconies, patios
with a lot of containers, vegetable gardens
and paved town gardens.

During hot weather pots need to be
watered once a day and hanging baskets
more frequently. This is extraordinarily
time-consuming, and is one of those jobs
which tends to be conveniently forgotten.
Unfortunately such forgetfulness is fatal to
the poor thirsty plants, which, in very hot
weather, will wilt away in a matter of
hours.

Although an automatic system may be
expensive to install, ultimately it will save
you money by ensuring that a mass of
plants are not wiped out at one go simply
because you are busy elsewhere or have forgotten to water them.

The simplest sort of automatic watering
system involves no more than an ordinary
sprinkler controlled by a computerised
timer. However in some areas where water
shortages occur, sprinklers are banned during certain months.

The alternatives are underground
sprinklers, trickle or drip feed systems.
Underground sprinkler systems consist of
PVC pipes which feed a network of hoses,
watering heads and sprinklers. Installing
such a system is complicated and should be
left to a specialist company. Trickle or drip
feed systems are excellent for terraces and
balconies and, in the open garden, for
borders or vegetable gardens. They are normally fitted in conjunction with a timer to
avoid wastage and with a removable filter
for cleaning.

Above
Climbers, trees and a garden bench help to disguise this shed.

practical buildings

Every gardener needs tools and associated equipment, such as pots, bags of compost, fertilisers and so on, as well as barbecues, garden chairs, parasols and play equipment. It follows that every gardener needs somewhere to keep all of this clutter. Any gardener keen on growing food will also find a greenhouse and potting shed indispensable.

sheds and storage

If your garden is large enough, a garden shed is more than a luxury, it is a necessity. Ideally it should be large enough to be a workshop and a place to pot up plants, with enough space left to store all your tools, children's toys and garden furniture.

When choosing a shed, check that it is solidly constructed and that the timber has been treated to withstand the weather –

pressure-treated timber is preferable to dipped timber. Check that the windows and doors open smoothly, the roof is strong and that it has gutters. The other important point is the floor, which will need a firm, flat foundation, such as paving or concrete.

Those with small gardens have more of a problem. Of course it is possible to set aside part of a large garage for gardening kit and there is always the under-the-stairs glory hole. However this is often reserved for coats, bags and golf clubs and being in the house is far from ideal. One solution is to build or buy benches with lift-up lids for the patio, to provide seating as well as storage space. There are also mini storage units and lean-to sheds with hinged lids and sliding doors just big enough for tools. These are usually made from pre-painted steel or fibre-glass.

greenhouses

Anyone with a family will be aware of all the additives in food and, if they have the space, will be anxious to grow their own fruit and vegetables. A greenhouse provides the best means of germinating your seeds.

There are two basic types of frame: wood or aluminium. Wood looks more traditional and rustic and so suits a period or country property better than aluminium. However the latter is far easier to maintain and keep clean.

Once you have decided on the sort of frame you want, you need to consider size. Work out what you intend to grow and how much space it will take up and then double it, as it is inevitable that you will be tempted to grow more. Buy sufficient ventilation and staging for your needs.

The site you choose will play a major part in determining your success. Sunshine is vital, so find a light, open position. You will also need easy access to water and possibly electricity, as you may wish to heat the greenhouse in winter, or use a propagator.

play time

While parents must be able, for safety reasons, to keep an eye on little children, older children need their own space where they are free to be adventurous. They love hidden corners, where they can play hide-and-seek, make dens and pretend they are fearless explorers, so site their play area in a far corner, or give them some feeling of privacy by planting a hedge or erecting a fence and covering it with climbers.

▶ choosing play equipment

Always buy the best quality you can afford, and always buy from a reputable dealer. Second-hand equipment may be cheaper, but, unless you are buying from a friend you can trust, you cannot be sure of its history or how it has been treated.

Check for sharp edges, protruding nails and screws and unplaned wood which may splinter. Ensure the equipment carries a kite mark to prove it has passed all the relevant safety tests. All countries run their own safety tests and have symbols to signify that a toy or piece of equipment has reached the recommended standard. In addition the European Union has its own safety symbol. Also check for age-recommended symbols as many pieces of equipment are not suitable for under-threes.

Regularly examine and maintain play equipment and structures. Make sure free-standing slides, climbing frames and swings are firmly anchored in the ground and that all nuts and bolts are still tight. Buy hard-wearing nylon rope in preference to traditional hemp, and replace it at the first signs of fraying.

Remember that children are imaginative and unpredictable, so will not necessarily use their play equipment in the way the manufacturer intended. A good general rule is always to expect the unexpected.

To be sure your children have a soft landing if they fall, place play equipment on well-watered grass, safety matting or,

even better, a thick layer of bark or wood chippings or sand. It is also advisable to choose a semi-shaded area for any play equipment or structures, so that children are not exposed for long periods to harmful ultraviolet rays.

water and sand

All children love sand and water. This classic sea-side combination offers endless opportunities to get wet and dirty, both popular pursuits, especially with the under fives. So paddling pools and sandpits will be well used.

If you have the space, a permanent sand play area is worth considering. This can take the form of a pit, or more simply, a box. You can always convert it into a flower bed, sunken herb garden or pool once the children have grown out of it.

For a simple sandpit dig a hole to the desired depth and width, spread a sheet of heavy-duty plastic, with holes punched in it for drainage, on the bottom, then fill with children's play sand (not builders' sand). Finish the sandpit with a low wall of pressure-treated wooden stockading, stone or brick. For a sandbox spread the plastic on the ground then use four railway sleepers as sides. Make sure that the sleepers are not heavily impregnated with tar, which will leak out in hot sunshine, making a sticky (and toxic) mess. There are also kits with ready-cut and planed wooden planks which slot together.

If you live near the sea, buy an old, holed dingy and use that as your sandpit. It will be very picturesque and look wholly in keeping with the setting.

Two of the most popular designs among the huge range of ready-made sandpits are the plastic boat and clam shell. These are made in two sections, forming a base and lid, which give much more scope for flexibility. For example, you can fill the base with sand and the lid with water.

Covers are very important for sandpits. They keep the sand dry, but more importantly keep it clean, preventing animals from fouling it. Use a sheet of fine mesh or oilcloth as a cover for home-made sand play areas, or fit a wooden lid, if the sandpit forms part of a decked area.

As with sandpits, there are paddling pools to suit all ages of children and size of garden – from little ones you blow up, through rigid moulded plastic, to large, soft, plastic pools with metal frames. Remember that regardless of the pool you choose, adult supervision is vital.

Water is such fun on a hot summer's day, so supplement their paddling pool with other water toys, such as bubble machines and water sprinklers. There is a range of random-spray, oscillating water sprinklers which fulfil every criteria for fun. They look bright and cheerful – being disguised as flowers, insects and animals – and produce a refreshing fine spray which will cool children down. Yet it is the surprise element which makes them so tremendously enjoyable. Even the most alert child is bound to be caught off-guard and given a soaking. Move the sprinklers around the garden and your plants will love them too.

Combine a random sprinkler with a water slide and you will find it almost impossible to drag the children indoors at bed time. For a simple slide, spread a large sheet of plastic or oil cloth on the ground and make it good and slippery with a sprinkling of water mixed with a few drops of washing-up liquid. If you want a really fast slide, place the plastic on a slight slope.

Above
Water is always a favourite with young children, and whether you have a water feature they can play in or simply fill an inexpensive paddling pool, they are bound to love it.

Right
A large pile of sand in a corner of the garden will suffice, but make sure you cover it with a sheet of fine mesh or oil cloth after use to ensure it stays clean and dry.

Above
Choose play equipment
that you can add to as
your child grows.
Walkways, cable runs
and rope ladders create
an adventure play-
ground heaven.

play structures

Giving children their own space and territory is important for their happiness as well
as good family relations. If everyone is on
top of each other irritations soon develop
and arguments are inevitable. Private hide-
aways and secret dens are an excellent way
of providing the sense of adventure and
freedom children require within the safety
of their garden.

Even before children learn to walk they
are trying to climb, pulling themselves
upright by any means available. So what
could be better than providing them with
the means to indulge this basic instinct.

Climbing frames range from the simplest
structure of two ends connected by a single
crossbar, to veritable labyrinths of ladders,
walkways, slides, swings, awnings and tun-
nels. Choose a frame that you can add to,
so that it grows with your children, constantly offering new challenges to their
developing abilities.

Give some thought to the material the
frame is made of as, once up, it will be a
feature in your garden for years to come.
There are many brightly-coloured metal
frames on the market, but there are also
more subdued wooden frames available,
with dark green attachments rather than
vivid red or orange.

If you are lucky enough to have a few
sturdy trees then you can attach climbing
ropes, rope ladders, commando-style net-

ting and swings to their branches and you
have the most natural frame there could be.

Even if you cannot find the space for a
climbing frame it is always possible to fit in
a swing – there are even models which can
be attached to the wall of a house, if you
have a tiny courtyard garden. Of all play
apparatus, swings are unique in that they
are equally popular with boys and girls,
toddlers and teenagers.

If you do not have a suitable tree, buy
or make a frame instead. Self-assembly
aluminium or wooden frames are not
expensive and are easy to erect, the only
tricky bit being anchoring the legs. These
can be secured by pins, but the safest
method is to sink them in concrete-filled
holes several feet deep.

Make your swing grow with your child by
altering the seat. Babies require a high-
backed bucket seat with a safety harness
and restraining bar at the front. The next
stage up is the strap, or belt seat made
of soft rubber which moulds itself to the
shape of the child's bottom, preventing
them from slipping off. For seven year olds
and upwards there is the flat rubber or
planked seat.

Both children and grown-ups can get a
very nasty injury if they are hit by a moving swing, so place the swing well away
from paths, sandpits and playhouses and
drill into your children the importance of
keeping their distance – you can always
mark out an exclusion zone.

trampolines

Young children will love sit-on, bouncy,
rubber balls and small trampolines, and for
older children with masses of energy a full-
size trampoline is tremendous.

Ensure one child or an adult keeps watch
while another bounces and fit cushioned pads
to cover the hard edges of the frame. If you
follow a few safety guidelines – one at a time,
no shoes or jewellery, no eating and drinking
– your children will bounce happily for hours.

▸ p l a y h o u s e s

Anyone who read *Peter Pan* when young will have been enchanted by Wendy's little house and yearned for one of their own. Wendy houses, now generally called playhouses, are still popular, as are tents, wigwams, tree-houses and dens.

There are many delightful, ready-made playhouses available, some with window boxes, little verandahs and even upstairs rooms. To add to the charm of these buildings, paint or colour-stain them a soft blue-grey or any colour that ties in with your overall scheme and decorate simply, with gingham curtains and a few pots of cheerful pelargoniums.

If you have an old shed that you do not use often you can transform it into a woodland cabin straight out of the fairy tale 'Hansel and Gretel'. Cut logs into thin cross-sections or split larch poles lengthways and nail them to the outside walls. To complete the picture, plant ivy to swarm up the sides and a mass of striking leafy plants, such as *Euonymus* or ferns, to disguise the entrance and add to the feeling of mystery.

Alternatively create a Heidi-inspired look by cutting Tyrolean-style ornamental eaves and shutters out of marine ply and fixing them on to the shed. Add some window boxes, hang checked curtains at the windows and colour-stain or paint.

If your shed is in a very leafy corner of the garden you could try a jungle theme. Attach bamboo screens to the sides of the shed and disguise the roof with a thatch screen, made from woven brushwood. Plant a couple of Fatsia japonicas – which have large, glossy, tropical-looking leaves – and place a cut-out painted plywood tiger so that it is peeping out from behind the vegetation.

No child will be able to resist the charm of a living, albeit temporary, playhouse made from sunflowers and woven willow or hazel switches. Plant the sunflowers, willow or hazel in a circle, leaving a space for an entrance. As the sunflowers grow, their huge heads form a natural roof with the willow and hazel. However, you will need to tie the tops together once they have reached a suitable height. To create a living playhouse that will look just as good in winter as summer use evergreens.

tents and wigwams

A garden takes on a completely different atmosphere at night. Children are fascinated by the way darkness transforms the garden, making it almost an alien territory, complete with strange rustlings and calls.

Above
A little hidden area
serves the same pur-
pose as a playhouse –
as long as children
can escape from their
parents for a while,
they'll be happy!

To really appreciate this you have to spend a night outside and the best way to do this is in a tent.

There is something very appealing about sleeping under canvas, with only a sheet of thin fabric between you and the stars. It is something every child should be allowed to experience. To avoid frustration, choose a small, simple-to-erect tent, hard-wearing enough to withstand daytime play, so that you will be able to use it as a portable playhouse.

If you have a child approaching their eighth, ninth or tenth birthday and you are stuck for what to do, invite a couple of his or her best friends to an out-of-doors sleep-over, complete with birthday barbecue. No one will get much sleep, but it will be an unforgettable night.

Sometimes it is best to keep things simple and in the case of wigwams this is definitely so. Children will get just as much enjoy-ment from a wigwam made from bamboos or hazel poles and an old sheet they have painted themselves, as from the smartest shop-bought offering. However if your gar-den is large why not build a permanent wigwam which can double as a climbing frame and later as a support for climbing plants.

You will need five treated timber poles for the frame. These of must be buried a couple of feet in the ground, preferably concrete for extra stability, then secured at their tops by threading thin, metal, wire hawser through holes drilled for the pur-pose. Once in place, hang a climbing rope from the top of the wigwam and wrap more rope around the sides. Fling an old sheet or blanket over the top when the children want to use it as a hideaway.

treehouses

Build your children a treehouse and you will covet it so much that you will not be able to wait until bedtime, when at last you can climb into it to enjoy an early evening drink as the sun slowly sets.

The type of treehouse you build will be determined by the type and shape of the tree you wish to use. You may be fortunate enough to have a mature tree with three or four thick branches spreading out from the main trunk. If so then these will form a wonderfully stable foundation on which to build. However it is more likely that you will need to use wooden posts as supports (sunk a few feet into the ground and buried in concrete), so that the house is virtually self-supporting, although it appears to be sitting up in the tree. Whichever tree you select for a treehouse, make quite sure that its boughs are healthy and strong and that there is no danger of breaking branches from above.

The distance from the treehouse platform to the ground is crucial. Obviously if your children are very little you will not want them climbing too high. You must also be sure that the ladder is firmly secured, its treads are not too far apart, and it is not set at too steep an angle. Rope ladders are not suitable for little children.

If the children are really young you could buy a large wooden dog kennel, cut out holes for windows, glaze them with shatter-proof plastic, paint it a pretty colour and place it in a low-growing tree, such as an apple. It may need extra supports but its fully-enclosed sides make it extremely safe.

Treehouses for older children can be higher and more open and, if the tree allows it, you could build more than one platform or storey. Use well seasoned, treated timber for the supports, base and cross beams, making sure that it is smooth and splinter free. Floors, walls and roofs can be made from sheets of marine ply with the roof covered with shingles or roofing felt. The outside of the treehouse can be softened and camouflaged with woven hazel hurdles or clap boarding. You could set up a rope and pulley, so you can replen-ish provisions!

▶games

If you use your garden as an outside room, then almost anything goes. If your child has a favourite toy, then encourage them to take it outside, if the weather is fine.

games for the family

There are many traditional games in which all the family can join. Bat and ball games such as cricket, baseball, rounders and French cricket have delighted generations of children.

Similarly, games requiring a racket, such as badminton and swing ball, will provide hours of entertainment and exercise as well as helping children to concentrate and develop their hand-eye coordination.

Croquet and boules, while more leisurely are just as popular, and are particularly good for the cool of evening, when you are trying to get everyone to wind down.

Even if you live in the country there is no reason why your children need miss out on such traditional street games as hopscotch. They can simply mark out their squares in chalk on any paved area – the chalk will wash off as soon as it rains. More permanent hopscotch, chess, or draughts boards can be made from coloured paving slabs (see Chapter 2).

eating alfresco

Summertime alfresco meals conjure up their own unique ambience. From the promise of a long, heat-hazy day at breakfast time, through to starry evenings among the heady fragrances of night-scented plants, the atmosphere of the garden alters as no interior space can. Whether you enjoy sophisticated, elegant, adult supper parties or cheerful, noisy, family barbecues, the garden as dining room provides a setting for some truly memorable occasions.

▸dining outdoors

As with all your garden furnishings your dining furniture should tie in with house and garden style and must suit your needs in terms of sturdiness and ease of storage.

Below
An all-in-one picnic table is inexpensive and very stable – ideal for a family garden.

Each material has advantages and disadvantages (see Chapter 3) but your first consideration should be the number of people will you need to seat.

If you cannot find a large enough table within your price range, why not dress up an ordinary table. Office supply shops often have large, sturdy tables with metal legs and wooden tops which are perfectly adaptable for garden use. Choose a colour such as dark green, which always looks good out of doors and then paint the legs and stick matching tiles on the tabletop. The result is extremely stylish and will easily cope with summer showers, although a plastic cover is advisable for winter.

deciding where to dine

The position of your dining area will determine how often you use it. If it is too far from the kitchen, eating out will be too much of an effort, however if the area closest to the kitchen happens to be without shade, exceptionally windy or down a precipitous flight of steps, this option is equally unappealing.

Comfort is all important when it comes to eating out. Everyone must feel relaxed and the dining area must be spacious enough for people to be able to push their chair back at the end of the meal to chat, cuddle little children on their laps or just enjoy the garden. As a general rule an area 3.6m/ 12ft square should be sufficient.

Shade is also vital. Lunch under a blazing sun takes on the characteristics of an endurance test rather than being the relaxed unhurried affair it should be. Even breakfast can be intolerable if the sun is beating down, hurting your eyes and melting the butter.

If your garden has no natural shade, buy a canvas parasol or canopy or, for a really beautiful setting, build an arbour over which you can train climbers.

setting
the scene

Right
Positioning a water fea-
ture near your dining
area will provide an
atmospheric back-
ground sound while
you eat.

Right
Positioning a water fea-
ture near your dining
area will provide an
atmospheric back-
ground sound while
you eat.

Below
Choosing tablecloths
that coordinate with
your favourite plants
will enhance your
dining area.

Once you have picked the ideal site,
set about turning it into a spot where
people will want to linger. Containers
really come into their own here.
Gather together a group of different
shapes and sizes and fill them with a
good variety of plants. Include some
flowering shrubs and small trees –
such as *camellia*, peony and a pretty
miniature Japanese maple – to provide
a permanent framework, then fill in
with tubs or pots of spring and sum-
mer-flowering bulbs, a froth of
Nemesia, daisy-like *Argyranthemum*
or colourful *pelargonium*.

Be sure to include some containers of herbs
that can be plucked as instant flavourings
or garnishes. And for a post-prandial
snack, place a couple of terracotta strawberry pots where diners can reach out and
pick the fruit, or plant wild strawberry
plants between cracks in the pavers or
along the edges of surrounding beds. In
warm climates a grape vine (*Vitis vinifera*)
adds exotic shade and provides a ready-
made dessert.

Think of your outdoor dining area as a
theatrical stage set, to be re-dressed as the
mood takes you. One of the joys of containers is that they can be moved around and
replanted easily, so you can constantly
change and update your colour scheme and
create more or less dramatic effects. If you
change your table covering and china you
can transform the setting of the meal.

Vary the look of your table by leaving it
uncovered for breakfast, covering it with a
cheerful gingham tablecloth for lunch, a
colourful oilcloth for children's tea, then a
dark tablecloth for the grown-ups' supper.
Once in a while you can make a real occa-
sion out of supper and go all out to create
an evening of high drama and glamour.
Dress the table with crisp white linen, glint-
ing silver cutlery and sparkling polished
glass, light it with candelabra and lanterns
and you will have a stylish and elegant setting for a dinner party.

▶a feast for all the senses

Once your visual sense is satisfied do not neglect to feed the other senses. To make your dining area complete use the power of scent, sound and touch.

Sound brings an area to life. The tinkle of running water creates a magical ambience, so try to incorporate a simple wall fountain or bubble pond near to where you plan to eat. The faint, rather mystical music of wind chimes will also add to the atmosphere as long as your garden is not windy, in which case the sound can be tortuous. The rustle of bamboo grasses or broad-leaved plants such as hostas add their own contribution to the garden sounds.

Fill the air with perfume from container-grown plants such as scented leaf *Pelargonium* (*P*. 'Graveolens' or *P*. 'Fragrans' are lovely), stately lilies (such as *Lilium regale* or *longiflorum*), and tobacco plants (*Nicotiana alata*). Train climbers such as honeysuckle, jasmine, *Solanum crispum* or the roses 'New Dawn' or 'Madame Alfred Carriére' up any vertical surface and plant fragrant shrubs such as mock orange (*Philadelphus*), Mexican orange (*Choisya ternata*) or *Viburnum* (*V. carlesii*) nearby.

Finally add some containers of velvet-petalled pansies to stroke and place a few pots of silky ornamental grasses strategically, where you can run your fingers through them in passing. They will also rustle in a breeze.

Right
The *Ranunculus* in the vase and the *Clematis montana* on the trellis perfume this eating area, and coordinate beautifully with the colour of the table.

Below
Blackberries grown around this seated area provide a convenient dessert. Small trees in containers give privacy.

informal eating

Try to drag yourself away from your wonderful dining area from time to time, to experience the joys of eating somewhere totally different. This may be underneath a spreading tree or in a quiet corner where the garden looks quite different.

Above
A table, stools, cushions and toys on the lawn provide a relaxed and practical setting for children to enjoy eating and playing in the sun.

For truly informal eating, fling down a rug, or set up a circle of tree stumps as little stools for the children to have an elfin feast. Children's parties work well out of doors. There is no need to worry about spilt drinks or twenty pairs of little hands smearing chocolate all over the walls.

Prepare a picnic basket with individual packets of sandwiches and fruit to avoid disagreements and remember that eating out-of-doors does something miraculous to children's appetites. The daintiest little eater will become a ravenous creature.

Hide little treats around the garden for the children to seek after lunch. This will keep them nicely occupied while the grown-ups settle down to their meal. Keep a few of the treats in reserve in case any child snaffles too many and leaves someone empty-handed and tearful.

barbecues

Eating out-of-doors is even more fun if you cook alfresco as well. There's nothing better than a party of family and friends gathered around tables laden with salads and delicious bread and being tortured by the delicious smells of meat, fish and vegetables cooking on the barbecue.

Barbecues fall into two different basic types, built-in and free-standing. Within the second category are numerous different electric and gas-powered models for those who cannot stand mess, or the traditional charcoal-fuelled barbecue – the only choice for the real aficionado.

Free-standing barbecues vary enormously in size, weight and therefore portability. There are excellent small cast iron models which can be placed on a wall or bricks and which are ideal for a couple of people, or for picnics. For a family, a larger brazier, kettle or, for really serious barbecuers, rotisserie grill, are more suitable.

It is a simple matter to build your own permanent barbecue. To decide on a site, take into account the direction of the prevailing wind, distance from the kitchen and outdoor dining area, and safety. You will need stone or frost-proof bricks for the three walls and base, and a metal brazier and metal grill tray. Design the barbecue so that the trays can be easily removed for cleaning, and include enough storage space for fuel, as well as flat surfaces to take all the utensils, dishes and bowls you will need while cooking.

Plant a mass of herbs around the base of the barbecue and if it looks a little forlorn in winter, disguise it with planted containers or an attractive, removable wooden lid.

Eating out-of-doors seems to enhance flavours, so the simplest food tastes quite delicious. Yet it is also fun to experiment with different themes. Thai, Caribbean, Mexican and Spanish foods all lend themselves especially well to barbecuing. Their spicy, tangy flavours are offset beautifully by the bitter-sweet smokiness that cooking over an open flame produces.

Good planning and timing are essential for success. Meat marinated overnight will be more tender and tasty, and certain foods benefit immeasurably from being started off in the oven. This is especially important for joints of chicken, as nothing is more off-putting and potentially dangerous than being handed a piece of chicken which is virtually black on the outside but still pink and bloody in the middle. Whether you

cook on charcoal or wood remember to allow sufficient time for the fuel to become hot enough for cooking.

Towards the end of cooking throw a few herbs or slivers of wet wood from fruit trees on to the barbecue to create deliciously aromatic smoke.

Certain barbecue foods are guaranteed to be a success with children. Sausages and kebabs are easy to eat as everything is already in bite-sized pieces and pork chops marinated overnight in crushed garlic, lemon juice and olive oil, will all be devoured by even the choosiest child.

Fresh fish barbecues well, especially swordfish and tuna that both have good solid flesh. Little sardines and mackerel are also quite delicious.

Always provide plenty of salads and bread. Other must-have's are coleslaw, potato salad, and a Greek salad made from tomatoes, cucumber and feta cheese in a piquant dressing.

Above
An example of a permanent barbecue. The surrounding low brick wall makes an ideal flat surface for cooking utentsils, dishes and seating.

▶garden lighting

Above
A partially concealed
spotlight is discreet
in the day and can be
angled to shine
through the grass to
highlight a feature.

Nothing has quite such an effect on atmosphere as lighting. An otherwise plain area can be made wildly romantic with cleverly placed lanterns and candles. Lighting can extend the period for sitting outdoors, can be used to highlight features – such as an interesting tree, fountain or statue – and extends your enjoyment of the garden for winter evenings when you are looking out from the warmth of the house.

Exactly as with interior rooms you should think of outdoor lighting fulfilling two basic purposes – one being utilitarian and the other decorative. The former is deployed for safety and security beside driveways, steps, pools, paths and dining areas while decorative lighting is used to illuminate interesting features and to provide atmosphere.

Plan the positions of utilitarian lights first, as they are often the simplest to place. Start with your parking and entrances to the house, then consider the dining area, and any steps and paths leading off it down which you may wander in the evening. Paths to a swimming pool, tennis court, coal or log store as well as the bin area, will need occasional lighting.

If security is a worry well-placed lights will deter intruders and help the householder feel safer. If you are worried about light pollution and saving energy then lights which switch themselves on when they sense movement are the answer. But be aware that dogs and cats may often trigger these.

Next turn your attention to decorative lighting. If you have a fantastic statue or urn it would make a perfect candidate to be picked out in a spotlight, and moving water or a gnarled old tree will also look spectacular. The angle of the lighting will give different effects. For example, backlighting produces dramatic silhouettes, uplighting picks out unusual features you would not notice during the day, while downlighting is closest to daylight.

For the dining area you will need more muted background lighting, to which you can then add, in keeping with the style of meal you are planning.

As with any electrical equipment, garden lighting should be installed by a qualified electrician. For a complex set-up armoured cables may need to be sunk into the ground. There are heavy-duty weatherproof cables available which can run along

Above
Candles are another option for outdoor lighting. Why not just move your indoor candles outside for an evening? Make sure they are not too near any foliage.

Right
Placing lights near steps makes moving around the garden at night much safer.

Left
A combination of uplighters, spot lights and candle light create a magical atmosphere, ideal for evening entertaining.

the surface and may be disguised with foliage or chippings. These are probably not a good choice for a family garden as they could trip someone, and if accidentally cut would give an electric shock.

The harsh glare of electric light can destroy the atmosphere of an outside dining area. It is impossible to relax when you are impaled by the glare of a spotlight. People are more at ease when the lighting is kept low – although if it is too dim you will find yourself peering uncomfortably at your plate in an attempt to work out just what is what. There are more subtle means of lighting your table, including lighting which 'grazes' the wall of the house, or gently uplights nearby foliage.

However, for alfresco suppers the ideal light is cast by candles. It is soft and flattering, the shadows are not as defined as those of electric light, and the candle-light has warmth and life to it.

Lanterns solve the problem of a breezy patio with guttering candles. There are old fashioned storm lanterns, hurricane lights, Indian-style brass lamps with star-shaped holes punched in them, or antique-style, glass, jam jars containing nightlights. These can sit on the table or hang from metal stakes stuck in the ground. The list of candle holders and protective containers is endless.

If you want to make the evening electricity-free from start to finish, guide your guests to the table along a pathway of large garden candles or paraffin-fuelled, oriental, bamboo torches stuck in the ground.

Many candles and lanterns perform a dual function – providing light while discouraging insects. The scent of citronella is delicious to humans but hated by insects and strangely insects find lanterns with orange-coloured glass less alluring than those with clear glass. There are also lanterns that emit ultra violet light. This attracts the insects and then electrocutes them as they land on the element. A few of these placed in a circle a discreet distance from the table should ensure a bite-free evening for everyone.

outdoor heating

Outdoor heaters and portable fireplaces have long been popular in Scandinavian countries. There are large, overhead, electric bar heaters and free-standing, portable, electric, convector models. But it is very easy to build your own outdoor hearth, or use a barbecue as a raised fireplace. If you really pile on the fuel and light it well before you eat, it should be red-hot by the time you sit down.

animals

Most children are fascinated by animals and if you can encourage this fascination you will not only give your children an interest that will stay with them for life, but one that is educational and will teach them about responsibility and caring for others.

▶ family pets

The size of your house and garden will help decide which animal is suitable for your family. A town house with a small courtyard garden is hardly the best place for a goat or enormous dog.

inside or out?

Certain pets are quite happy living out of doors for most of the year, depending on the severity of the climate. Rabbits and guinea pigs can cope with quite harsh weather as long as they have a water-tight, draught-proof hutch with plenty of bedding material to keep them snug. The hutch should have a large run attached as they like lots of exercise. Place the hutch in a sheltered part of the garden, where the animal will be protected from the worst of the weather.

Cats and dogs need access to a garden, but other pets such as rats, mice, gerbils and hamsters also enjoy an occasional trip outside. However they must be kept inside their cage otherwise they will soon vanish.

escape-proof garden

It is virtually impossible to make your garden totally escape-proof without surrounding it with a very high wire fence, with the base buried a good way underground. Cats, rabbits, pigs and goats are seasoned escapees. Equally foxes, deer, badgers and wild rabbits will nearly always be able to find a way in if they so desire. So never let domestic rabbits have free run of the garden and keep goats on a leash, but allow cats freedom to roam. To contain small livestock, a good thick hedge supple-

Below
You could disguise a kennel or hutch by training climbers over the top, to blend it into its surroundings.

mented with an electric fence should be sufficient. Do make sure the hutch is very secure – not only to stop your pets escaping, but to prevent any predators such as cats or foxes from getting at them.

hygiene

It's relatively easy to train dogs not to defecate on flowerbeds, but cats are a different matter. The best policy is to encourage them to use one particular area and to start this process when they are young kittens. Train them to use a litter tray, then when the weather gets warmer take the tray outside and find a suitable spot for it. Show the kitten the tray so it gets used to using it in that position, then one day dispense with the tray but spread some of the cat litter on the ground. The cat should keep on going back to the same spot, although be alert if you have gravel laid anywhere in the garden as they will find this very tempting. Larger sizes of gravel (2cm/1in and upwards) are more difficult for cats to scrape away.

If neighbours' cats are a problem, buy humane, plastic, spiky matting and place it under valued plants. Alternatively lay leaves and stems of prickly plants such as holly, mahonia, pyracantha and roses.

Toxoplasmosis is spread by cats and can be extremely dangerous, especially to pregnant women. So when gardening wear rubber or latex gloves underneath your gardening gloves and be sure to wash your hands thoroughly afterwards. Make sure that children also wash their hands well after they have been playing in the garden, and that everyone's tetanus cover is up to date.

If you find your plants under attack from wild animals then it is time to build defences. Kitchen gardens can be protected from rabbits with a chicken wire fence. Bury the base of this 30cm/1ft underground, and bend the wire for the same distance outwards at the very bottom to prevent the rabbits burrowing under.

Deer are altogether more difficult to deal with. They can jump very high, so fences, other than expensive high-tensile deer-proof fencing, are all but useless. The best thing to do is to try to protect individual plants or beds which are under attack. Garden centres sell pellets containing lion faeces, which when sprinkled around the plants keep some deer off. A less attractive method is to tie white plastic carrier bags to canes or tree branches at night. These will give the deer a fright and scare them off. However they will be back and will soon get used to the bags unless you keep moving them around. If deer are attacking young shrubs or trees, you will need wire barriers around them until they are fully grown.

Badgers and foxes can also cause quite a lot of damage to lawns as they dig holes to find grubs. Badgers are a protected species so must be left alone, however you can usually discourage foxes with pellets designed to deter cats and dogs.

Above
Rabbits make good pets and will be very happy in a large garden with space for a long run.

▶small farm animals

If you have the space and time to devote to them, it is immensely rewarding to keep a few small farm animals, either as pets or as livestock.

ponies

Taking on a pony is a huge and expensive responsibility and not to be embarked upon lightly unless you are absolutely sure your children will take on the daily discipline of mucking out, grooming, feeding and exercising. You may also find you need to buy a horsebox and give up countless weekends to go to gymkhanas and point-to-points. You not only need a paddock and stable, but tack, suitable clothing, and, of course,

feed. Vet's bills add to the costs. However, once children have caught the pony bug their enjoyment is so overwhelming and infectious, that parents cannot help but be won over.

goats

Goats are great fun and are useful to keep the grass shorn. They are easy to milk, and the milk makes fantastic cheese. Some sort of shed is vital if you want to keep goats as they are delicate creatures and must be taken in overnight, or if it is rainy or cold. They eat anything and everything, therefore should be kept in a secure paddock or on a strong tether, well out of reach of prized plants.

pigs

It is curious that pigs have such a bad reputation as they are intelligent creatures with great character and, contrary to popular belief are very clean. If you are only keeping a few pigs a small shed with a paddock or enclosed yard attached will be sufficient, as long as the shed is draught-free, warm and dry. Some pigs, such as Vietnamese pot-bellied pigs, are so affectionate that they have long been kept as pets. They can even be trained to use a litter tray.

sheep

Firstly consider whether you want to keep sheep purely as a hobby, in which case it may be fun to concentrate on a rare breed, or whether you want to keep them for their milk, wool, or meat. Once you have decided, you can set about choosing a breed, although do get expert advice before buying. Generally sheep are happy left to graze with little or no shelter besides that

Below
A dream pet for many children and one that will cost the parents a small fortune!

Right
Hens will be very happy kept in a garden, though they are best kept in a pen as they will eat everything in sight. Children will love feeding them and looking out for eggs.

provided by trees, hedges or rocks. If the climate is mild they can be left out all year, although in many places winters are so cold and wet that they will need to be brought indoors for the worst of it.

poultry

All poultry will attract predators such as foxes, so it is important to provide them with a secure house for night-time, surrounded by a strong, high fence. Remember that foxes can dig, so bury the fence approximately 46cm/18in and bend it outwards for the same distance.

geese

It is possible to get surprisingly attached to a goose. Although they are renowned as excellent watchdogs, certain breeds can be quite affectionate. One goose egg will provide enough scrambled eggs for two hungry people. They will also, if you have the heart for it, provide you with a traditional feast for Thanksgiving and Christmas.

ducks

An obvious requirement for ducks is access to water, whether a pond, a stream or even a large container for them to dunk their heads in. Ducks are comfortable-looking creatures and, like geese, provide delicious eggs and meat. They will not do much damage to flowers, but must be kept away from young vegetables. However, if you let them into the kitchen garden in autumn they are very helpful, gobbling up pests such as slugs. Both geese and ducks are liable to churn up the lawn and both leave large, messy droppings.

hens

Free-range eggs are so much better than the shop-bought variety, that for a growing family, hens are an excellent choice. Chickens and gardens do not mix as poultry is extremely destructive, so it is best to confine them in a run. They need green, leafy plants as well as grass to eat and plenty of grit in their diet. The ideal option is to allow them, like ducks, to graze the kitchen garden in autumn. If you have a portable hen house move this to the vegetable garden at the same time – this will allow the ground of their original run time to recover. You don't need to keep a cockerel in order for hens to lay eggs and sometimes the hens are happier without one around.

▶ a t t r a c t i n g
w i l d l i f e

Wildlife is more than an added attraction for a garden, it is vital for its well-being. Without insects and birds, plants would not be pollinated, seed would not spread so widely, and pests would thrive unhindered. Your garden would, in short, lack life, sound, movement and soul.

Above

An old tree covered with moss is a magnet for small insects and the animals that feed on them.

There is no reason why a garden attractive to wildlife should not also delight the human eye. For a wildlife garden does not need to be an untamed wilderness of brambles and weeds and can still look tidy without being overly manicured. Stop sweeping up each fallen leaf, burning every dead branch and mowing the grass with the blades set low and you will provide a huge range of creatures with suitable habitats and food without compromising beauty in any way.

There are various ways of creating a wildlife garden. If your garden is large enough, set aside one corner where the grass is allowed to grow longer (and so set seed) and plants are left to develop their berries and hips instead of being tidily pruned. A pile of logs rotting in a quiet corner, will attract a host of insects – which in turn will attract the small mammals and birds that feed off them.

Alternatively it is possible to work wonders simply by redesigning one border so that there is plenty of foliage and a range of nectar-rich flowers. Small creatures will love the protection the leaves provide, while insects will be attracted by the sweet nectar.

Where there are plentiful supplies of insects there will inevitably be numerous birds. Or you may decide to leave a few windfall apples on the ground for birds, badgers and any other hungry creatures.

If you possess a small city courtyard with no flowerbeds at all, don't despair. Fill containers with sweet-scented flowers and shrubs to perfume the air and act as a magnet for insects. And if you plant climbers such as ivy, honeysuckle, pyracantha and vines to scale the walls you will have created a vertical habitat – a tiny wildlife haven in the midst of all the concrete and fumes.

Similarly you don't need a large garden to put up a bat box. Bats are facing a rapid decline in their habitats, especially in Europe where old barns are being converted into houses, church towers and spires are being netted and lofts in houses are being made into extra rooms and the timbers sprayed with chemicals.

Whichever approach you decide to take, one of the keys to encouraging wildlife is to avoid the use of chemicals. However careful you are with these and however many assurances the manufacturers give as to their safety, they will inevitably get into the food chain and cause damage somewhere along the line.

The other key to a desirable wildlife environment is to plant native trees, shrubs and flowers that suit native wildlife.

If space allows, plant a hedge. Hedges look good and are a cheap and practical way of either marking your boundary or dividing up the garden. If you choose your shrubs carefully, aiming for a good mix of evergreen and deciduous, prickly and fine-leaved, you will provide an ideal habitat for all sorts of creatures.

Unfortunately in many countries the drive for ever greater agricultural yields along with the increasing size of machinery has encouraged farmers to grub up hedges to create enormous fields. Whenever this

happens a habitat which may have provided homes for countless insects, birds and
small mammals for generations is lost for
ever. By providing an alternative home for
all these creatures you will increase your
immediate enjoyment and have the satis-
faction of knowing that you are helping to
ensure that your children's children will
also be able to enjoy them. Remember
never to cut hedges during nesting time.

Another unexpected benefit to creating a
wildlife garden is that once established,
such a garden is low maintenance. The
increased number of birds and friendly
insects will happily gobble unwelcome visitors such as slugs, snails and aphids, so not
only will you have created an extra dimen-
sion to your garden, you will find it easier
to run.

Buy your children a pair of binoculars, a
magnifying glass, a couple of wildlife iden-
tification books and a nature diary, and
they will be kept happy and absorbed for
hours at a time.

▸birds

The sound of birds singing, whether the dawn chorus or the insistent melody of blackbirds marking out their territory at dusk, is one of the greatest delights.

Besides their wonderful song, birds' antics are extremely entertaining. Children and adults are equally fascinated by the sight of a thrush cracking open a snail's shell, a pair of sparrows trying to keep their nestful of hungry babies fed or a woodpecker's first flying lesson.

The two essential ingredients for life are food and habitat. Birds adore seeds, fruit, berries and insects, so choose trees, climbers and shrubs that will bear a good crop of berries – such as rowan (*Sorbus*), cotoneaster, pyracantha, berberis and holly. From seed, grow a selection of grasses and flowers with large seedheads and resist the temptation to cut them back in the autumn.

If you cultivate fruit and vegetables, set aside a few as an offering for the birds, either allowing them to bolt or leaving the plants unnetted. Feed birds indirectly by growing flowers which will attract insect prey, either by their smell, colour or the amount of nectar they produce.

Every year has its lean periods. Winter is obviously one of these, but spring and summer can occasionally be difficult too – spring because there is a period before the new fruits, seedheads or insects have appeared and summer because an exceptionally hot, dry period will leave the ground dry, so preventing insects from emerging. This is the time that birds will appreciate any help humans can provide.

There are various birdseed mixes available in the shops, however it is much more fun to devise your own menu for garden birds. Children particularly enjoy foraging

Right
A small birdbox nestled into your shrubs and trees rather than one sited in an exposed area, will attract birds.

Below
Bird seed combined with windfall apples hanging from a fence or trellis will attract a variety of different birds. By raising them off the ground you can keep the food away from predators.

for seeds and nuts and collecting suitable kitchen scraps, such as cereal, grated cheese and rice. Hang half coconuts and ripe seedheads around the garden. Sunflowers (*Helianthus*), with their enormous heads packed full of delicious seeds, are ideal for this. Bacon rinds cut into tiny pieces are also an enormous treat which will be snapped up in no time.

You may decide that rather than just throwing the birds' food on the ground, a birdfeeder or bird table is more convenient and tidier. Position the feeder or table where it can be seen from inside the house – preferably the kitchen window, as it is the most occupied room – yet not too close to where a cat might conceal itself. If there are a lot of squirrels in the area it is worth buying a squirrel-proof feeder or table to prevent them from raiding the birds' food.

Hygiene is important. Thoroughly clean the table or feeder regularly and discard any old food which might attract vermin or spread disease. Peanuts, for example, become poisonous if left to go soggy over several days of hot weather.

Feeding birds requires a certain commitment. If you start supplementary feeding in winter you must carry on throughout the season, as the birds will have started to rely on you and will quickly starve without your offerings. Another important point to remember is that whole peanuts can choke a baby bird and anything too fatty is extremely bad for their digestion, so do not put out food when the babies are hatching. Don't feed at nesting time as this detracts from nest-building.

Different birds like to feed in different ways and if you take this into account when you are setting out their food, you will avoid unseemly squabbles at the bird table. The larger ones may prefer perching on the table, the smaller, more acrobatic birds will happily eat swinging from a string suspended from a branch or even the table itself – much in the same way as they would feed clinging to a swaying strand of grass or a thin twig.

Water is an equally important requirement. Besides needing water to drink, birds use it for washing and grooming, vital for keeping their feathers in order. While it is important in summer when supplies may have dried up, it is important in winter when the birds' regular source may have frozen over. Most garden ponds are not much help as they tend to be too deep, and while it is possible to adapt a pond by piling large stones around the edge or building a ramp down into the water, it may be easier either to buy or to make a proper birdbath.

There are a vast number of designs on the market, from smart ornamental baths to very contemporary concrete styles. However it is great fun, and cheaper, to make your own. The simplest birdbath need consist of nothing more than an upturned dustbin lid. Children will find setting this up great fun. Simply place the upturned lid on a base of sand or a couple of old bricks to ensure it is flat and will not wobble, then sprinkle a few small stones or gravel in the bottom. If you wish, you could make it more aesthetically pleasing by

seed cake recipe

Use any mix of fat, seeds and nuts you like. Quantities are flexible, although the finished cake should be about the size of a tennis ball.

Ingredients:
• Selection of fats, such as suet, bacon fat, lard or dripping from roast meat
• Selection of seeds
• Selection of nuts (chopped finely)
• Dried fruit, such as currants or sultanas

1 Mix all the fats together and knead into a ball.
2 Roll the fat ball in the seeds, nuts and dried fruit, thoroughly coating it.
3 Using a long, thick, carpet darning needle thread the twine through the centre of the ball.
4 Tie a knot in one end of the twine and fashion a loop in the other end. Your bird seed cake is now ready to hang in the garden. Alternatively you can suspend it in the plastic netting used for supermarket fruit such as oranges.

Above
Birds need food in winter, especially if the ground is frozen.

Below
A bird table with a roof will provide shelter for birds from inclement weather and will prevent the food from being covered with snow or rain.

arranging a few large stones around the edge. These will also allow bees and other insects to drink without drowning. Change and replenish the water occasionally.

As with any water feature, if you have a very young family don't let them go near the bath unsupervised. Little children can drown in the tiniest amount of water.

habitat

The nesting requirements of different species of birds are very diverse. Some love holes in old trees, others dense foliage, such as that provided by shrubs, hedges, or climbers like ivy.

It is possible to attract a wide variety of birds, from owls to tits, by putting up a range of nest boxes. Like birdbaths there are many different styles available, from thatched rustic to Shaker style. It is also possible to buy traditional and rather grand white-painted pigeon- or dovecotes, which can either be fixed on the side of a building, or set on a post and left freestanding.

Whether you decide to buy a box or construct your own make sure that it is water-tight and remember that it is the size of the entrance which will determine which bird uses it.

It is important to choose the correct spot to site your box, otherwise the birds will simply shun it. Pick a place where it is not exposed to direct sunlight and where a cat cannot reach it – at least 3m/10ft above ground on a tree trunk, wall or fence.

Once the box is in place leave it well alone for the birds to find it. The only thing you can do to encourage them, besides making sure there is a good supply of food nearby, is to provide nesting material. This could be dry grass cuttings, fluffy pampas grass, thistledown and small twigs.

Once the birds are happily settled it's important not to disturb them too much. It is fine very quietly to peep into the box every once in a while, but beware of scaring them off, especially when they have little babies. It is much better to watch their comings and goings from a distance.

Once the babies have grown up and flown the nest the box will need to be cleaned out and disinfected. This is an excellent opportunity for children to examine the nest. They will find dissecting it totally fascinating but discourage them from taking the nest indoors as it may well be full of mites and fleas.

When you have cleaned out and thoroughly aired the box, sprinkle some clean hay or a few wood shavings inside it and leave it for the next occupants.

Occasionally you may see a newborn bird on the ground. While it seems lost it has probably just fallen out of its nest, which is bound to be just above it. First find the nest, then gently scoop up the little bird and put it back. However if the baby is a bit older and has feathers, do not touch it. Simply observe from a distance and scare off any predators, as the mother is probably close by and may even be teaching it to fly.

If you are really keen on birds it is not a good idea to have a cat. They are natural hunters and will not be able to stop themselves going after each and every bird which braves your garden. You cannot chastise this instinctive behaviour but it can be distressing to see creatures killed for sport.

▶ pond wildlife

Give any child a fishing net, jam jar and magnifying glass, then let them loose to explore a pond or boggy area and they will be in seventh heaven. But however delighted your children may be with a pond, the local wildlife will be even more so.

Below
The combination of a pond and luscious green plants makes a rich habitat for insects, birds, fish and small animals.

While some people think of a pond only in terms of fish, it will attract a wide range of creatures from insects and birds to small mammals and amphibians, all drawn to the pond to drink, wash and breed. In fact although fish are attractive, if you can resist buying them you will find that your pond becomes a richer habitat, as fish eat frog spawn. If you are really keen on fish choose those that are happiest in an indoor tank and then you and your children will be able to enjoy watching the pond for the magical metamorphosis from spawn to tadpole to frog. And as frogs eat slugs, snails and other garden pests they are definitely to be encouraged. You may also be fortunate enough to witness a new dragonfly, as it emerges from its case in early summer.

There are various ways you can make a pond more attractive and accessible to a variety of wildlife. Most ornamental ponds are designed with quite steep sides and edged with stone or concrete slabs. It is all too easy for little creatures to fall in then find themselves unable to clamber out. The hard surround may also become burning hot at the height of summer, forming an impenetrable barrier to many creatures.

All these drawbacks are easily surmounted. As to the problem of the steep sides, place a plank covered with chicken wire (to prevent it becoming slippery) so that it slopes down into pond, making a gentle ramp for birds and little creatures to descend safely. Alternatively you could collect together some large stones and pile them in the corner of the pond to form a more natural-looking escape route.

The problem of the baking hot edging slabs is overcome by growing a selection of leafy plants to provide shade and keep the paving cool. They will also provide natural cover for wildlife approaching the pond.

If you have very young children and are worried about the safety aspects of a pond, create a marshy or boggy area instead. This will attract wildlife, yet will be much safer.

Above
A bog garden is very
easy to create and it
will provide a home
for a wide variety of
wildlife.

To make a bog garden lay a sheet of pond liner over a shallow dip (a maximum of 60cm/2ft deep), punch a few holes in it, then cover the bottom with a layer of gravel. Now fill with soil, water well to ensure the soil settles and is really sodden, then plant up. A good thick layer of mulch will stop the water from evaporating too fast and help the plants establish themselves.

Once you have managed to attract a number of amphibians to your garden, keep them there by ensuring they have plenty of places to hibernate. A pile of logs or stones is ideal. Toads love long grass in the summer, as it stays cool and damp and offers plenty of cover. However the fact that they cannot be seen makes them vulnerable to harm, especially from mowers. Tiny new frogs also start to migrate away from the pond and across the lawn, so always check long grass before mowing at this time.

▶ butterflies, bees and other insects

Every garden has a wide selection of insects, some more welcome than others. High on the list of the 'goodies' of the insect kingdom are bees, whether honey or bumble, and hoverflies, dragonflies, lacewings and ladybirds. So if your insects tend to be of the pest variety it is worth making an effort to attract some of the more friendly kinds.

Below
Do not forget to plant *Buddleia davidii* – this is so popular with butterflies that it is commonly called the butterfly bush.

However many insects you have in the garden you can never have enough butterflies. It is not only their beautiful colours and prettily shaped wings which are appealing; their delicate fluttering flight is attractive.

Luckily the flowers that butterflies adore are just as pretty and so are worthy of a place in any garden. The only possible exceptions are nettles, which most gardeners try to eradicate altogether. However nettles are very important for many varieties of butterfly as they lay their eggs on the leaves. So if you want to have beautiful butterflies gracing your garden it is worth gritting your teeth and allowing a clump of nettles to grow in some out-of-the-way corner.

The other point to remember is that butterflies, being light-bodied insects, cannot stand the wind and prefer sunny, sheltered spots. So if your garden is quite windswept it is worth growing a hedge as a windbreak. When you have created your suntrap, either dig out a bed, or group together a selection of containers planted with colourful, fragrant plants. You will not only have a butterfly garden but a delightful place to eat out or simply sit and enjoy the comings and goings of the insects.

The needs of bees and other helpful insects are very similar to those of butterflies. They too are drawn to colourful, fragrant, nectar-rich flowers. Nectar is absolutely vital to the well-being of many flying insects as it provides them with energy-giving carbohydrates.

Herbs are also guaranteed to attract butterflies, bees and hoverflies, none of which can resist their strong aroma. Plant lavender, sage, thyme, rosemary and mint for fragrance, beauty and a host of attractive visitors. Other good choices are traditional cottage garden-style flowers such as catmint (*Nepeta*), sunflower (*Helianthus*), Aster, *anemone*, globe thistle (*Echinops ritro*) and *sedum*. Many insects, including butterflies and bees, find blue flowers particularly alluring, so include plenty of these when planning a butterfly/insect corner. Like birds, butterflies and other insects love to feed on rotting fruit, as it ferments, so leave some windfalls.

plants

It is quite astonishing how different plants can alter the look of a garden and, by so doing, the house attached to it. Apart from the joys of colour, perfume, sound and texture, this is one of the most exciting things about a garden – the opportunity they give their owners to display their personality decisively.

A look around any modern housing development will confirm this. Although all the houses and their plots may be identical on paper, the hard work and imagination their owners expend on their gardens transforms them, making each as individual as can be. One garden may show a Japanese influence, with raked gravel, bamboos and wind chimes exuding a thoroughly modern atmosphere of Zen-like calm, simplicity and control, while immediately next door a profusion of country cottage-style planting creates a timeless feeling of cheerful abundance.

▶gardening for children

Children may start off full of enthusiasm for gardening but if they fail to get results, or the results take too long to appear, they will quickly become disillusioned and lose interest. To ensure this does not happen it is vital to give them a good set of tools, a sheltered sunny site, and good soil in which things will grow well.

Don't try to palm them off with a dry, shady corner which you can't think of anything else to do with. If you encourage a love of gardening when your children are young it will stay with them for a lifetime.

Once you have chosen a mutually agreeable site, help your child to prepare it. Make sure the soil is well conditioned, adding compost and manure as necessary and do the heavy digging yourself.

When the children are choosing what to plant, gently direct them away from anything that requires too much attention and suggest they select mainly fast-growing, hardy plants, with a few playful ones, such as snapdragons (*Antirrhinum*), thrown in for fun.

To get the garden started buy some bedding plants, such as pretty *Lobelia*,

experiment with any number of strange colours or combination of plants.

Some dramatic plants will not go amiss. Children will delight in the enormous girth of pumpkins and the fantastic colours and strange shapes of gourds. Giant vegetables such as walking stick cabbages are great fun, while the ultimate novelty in any garden must be giant sunflowers, which can reach massive heights. Very little children may find these just too tall and may have more fun with smaller varieties closer to their own height. These will be more manageable, yet still tall enough to create an *Alice in Wonderland* feel.

When choosing packets of seed, steer children towards plants with large seeds that are easy to handle and can be relied on to give a good display, such as nasturtium (*Tropaeoleum*) and sunflower (*Helianthus*).

Other flowers which grow well from seed are the ever-popular sweet pea (*Lathyrus*) – an excellent choice as they love to be cut – marigolds (*Calendula*), love-in-a-mist (*Nigella*), (*Papaver*), cornflowers (*Centaurea cyanus*) and foxgloves (*Digitalis*). In fact foxgloves are a must for any child brought up on the stories of Beatrix Potter. Many

Above
Foxgloves grow exceptionally well from seed and have a particular relevance to any child brought up on Beatrix Potter.

Top Left
Allocate a large container as a garden for your child to look after.

Bottom Left
Help your child with the initial planting, and do it in stages, so it doesn't seem too much like hard work.

Right
A young child will have hours of fun with their own miniature wheelbarrow and tools – even if they don't actually do any gardening!

Begonia, *Petunia* or vivid *Zinnia* and pansy. These can be put in pots, used to edge the beds, or planted up to spell out the child's name.

Give children full rein when it comes to choosing colours. They may choose vivid, clashing combinations, but it is important that they feel their patch is truly theirs if they are really going to develop an enthusiasm. So grown-ups must allow them to

roses

Many roses are unsuitable for a family garden because of their thorns. Here is a selection that will be kinder to small fingers:

Thornless
Rosa 'Zéphirine Drouhin' Deep, magenta pink, perfumed flowers. Long summer to autumn flowering period. Is best on a north-facing wall.
R. 'Kathleen Harrop' A lovely fragrant climber with shell-pink flowers.
R. 'Goldfinch' A vigorous rambler which produces small, creamy-yellow blooms in summer.

Just the odd thorn
R. 'America' Vigorous climbing rose with large coral pink flowers. Lovely spicy fragrance and long flowering period.
R. 'Souvenir du Dr Jamain' A climber with deep, purple blooms and a very strong fragrance. Likes shade.
R. 'Ghislaine de Feligonde' A rambler that flowers all year, with apricot-coloured blooms. Any thorns will be on the back of the leaves.

nurseries and garden centres sell seed mixes especially formulated for children and these generally offer excellent value for money.

A few bulbs are always a good addition to any garden, as they are extremely undemanding and children are fascinated by the way these lifeless-looking, papery, underground parcels suddenly burst into bloom. Any selection should include a few early spring bulbs to build up anticipation for the start of the gardening year, as well as some which flower in autumn as a final flourish to round off the season.

Excellent spring bulbs are *Scilla*, *Iris reticulata*, grape hyacinth (*Muscari*) and of course that harbinger of spring, the crocus. All these bulbs produce small flowers that are extremely sweet and appeal to children's love of the miniature. Reliable autumn performers include many varieties of *Crocus*, *Colchicum*, *Sternbergia*, *Nerine* and *Cyclamen*; although all of these are small, and very delicate-looking they are actually extremely tough.

Once the children's garden is planted they should not feel you are constantly inspecting their efforts and interfering.

Left

Left
Lavender is a versatile and easy plant. It will grow happily in a container or in a flower bed and many varieties are hardy so can be left out all winter. You could pick the stems and flowers to make lavender bags.

Right
Whatever the weather, children will enjoy getting outside, even helping with everyday jobs such as digging and removing weeds.

Below
A willow pyramid placed over a box plant (*Buxus*) makes an interesting focal point in a flower bed.

how to make a pyramid

An interesting project for an older child is a topiary pyramid. However, this must only be undertaken with adult supervision as it involves using garden shears. Pyramids look extremely impressive flanking a flight of steps or a bench or positioned in a border as a focal point.

You can use privet (*Ligustrum*), box (*Buxus*), yew (*Taxus*), rosemary (*Rosemarinus*), hornbeam (*Carpiuus betulies*) or holly (*Ilex*).

1 Take eight small garden canes or willow switches and lash the frame together with twine.

2 Spread the canes or switches to form a pyramid.

3 Plant your chosen shrub in a pot or in a bed, then place the frame over it, pushing the canes down into the soil.

4 As the plant grows larger its shoots will start to push through the pyramid. Trim these back.

5 Once the plant has grown large enough to fill the frame, simply pull the pyramid off.

although a little discreet help, such as occasional watering, will probably be appreciated.

Children have extremely good senses and will particularly appreciate plants which have satisfying scents, colours, textures or even sounds.

Whether it be the rustling of bamboo stems and leaves, or whispering of ornamental grasses. This has a particularly strong appeal. Children's hearing is much more sensitive than adults and many young children can hear the high-pitched navigational squeaks of bats that are totally beyond an adult's hearing range.

Touch is also an important sense. Children love plants that have interesting textures or strokable flowers, leaves or bark. Silver, velvety-leaved lamb's tongue (*Stachys byzantina*), fluffy fennel (*Foemiculum vulgare*) and wormwood (*Artemesia*) or the silky petals of tulips are all popular. Many trees appeal to a child's

sense of touch. The pussy willow (*Salix caprea*), has fluffy catkins, the Himalyan silver birch (*Betula utilis jacquemontii*) and Chinese cherry (*Prunus serrula*), both have wonderful satiny bark, while the bark of the maple variety *Acer griseum* is as thin as fine paper and can be peeled off without harming the tree.

Anyone who has witnessed the uncanny ability of children to track down a piece of chocolate wherever it is hidden in the house, will testify to their powerful sense of smell. The garden offers endless opportunities for enticing smells and fragrances that are attractive to young noses.

They will revel in the heady smell of the white tobacco plant (*Nicotiana alata*) that releases its fragrance at dusk. Sweet rocket (*Hesperis matronalis*) and stock (*Matthiola*) are guaranteed to delight with their smells as sweet as cachous.

For more unexpected smells encourage children to plant chocolate cosmos (*Cosmos atrosangiuneus*). Besides its unusual dark flowers and velvety petals it releases a strong smell of chocolate. However, this is a tender perennial that needs a sheltered, frost-free and sunny position. The curry plant (*Helichrysum italicum*) is also surprising with its distinct unexpected aroma of curry.

Encourage children to collect lavender flowerheads, rose petals and other aromatic flowers and herbs. These can be dried and made into lavender bags, pot pourri or ribbon-tied bunches of culinary herbs, which they can give away as presents.

A really exciting present to grow which would impress even the most sophisticated adult, is false topiary. These pieces look astonishingly difficult to produce, but are actually deceptively simple. To produce a spiral, bird, or other similar small design buy a ready-made wire frame for it to climb. As the ivy grows it will cover the frame, eventually hiding it altogether.

Above
Chocolate cosmos: the name alone will interest children, and it also smells of chocolate!

Above
Snowdrops will be one of the first flowers to appear each year.

Right
Lamb's tongue has wonderful silky leaves which children will love stroking.

Far right
Ornamental grasses add interest because they rustle in the breeze.

▶herbs, fruit and vegetables

The wonderful thing about fruit, vegetables and herbs is that there is a variety to suit every situation, whether it's a small pot on a windowsill or a vast allotment. Even if your family possess just a tiny balcony, your children can enjoy the pleasure of growing and harvesting their own crop.

Below
Nothing compares to the taste of freshly harvested fruit, vegetables and herbs, so if you have room, try to set aside a piece of garden for growing your own supplies.

Aside from the health issues, and the fact that nothing compares with the taste of really fresh produce, there is something almost primitive about the thrill of plucking a piece of fruit off a tree or digging up some home grown vegetables. It is a thousand times more exciting than a trip to the supermarket and a pleasure that remains undiminished by repetition.

Children derive huge pleasure from harvesting fruit and vegetables. It is so satisfying filling a basket with your own produce, and the way root vegetables, such as potatoes and carrots, appear as the soil is turned is magical to a child.

designing a kitchen garden

Some people like to grow their fruit and vegetables in neat, regimented ranks, while others prefer to spice the design up a bit by digging out unusual-shaped beds, such as those found in a potager.

The word potager originated in France, where herbs, vegetables and flowers have long been grown together. The beauty of a potager does not stem solely from what is grown, but from the way it is laid out.

The design may be a simple grid pattern of four square beds with gravel, brick or grass paths between, or a more complicated geometric look – perhaps a circle, with segments radiating out from a centrepiece, such as a sundial or obelisk.

So the advantage of a potager is that it looks ornamental rather than simply utilitarian. It is possible to make such an attractive design that it is worth positioning it where it can be seen from the house. It's

especially useful in a small space where there is no room for a separate vegetable garden, an upper window from where the patterns of the beds can be appreciated to the full.

growing edible plants

Everyone has their favourite fruit and vegetables, but as a general rule it is a good idea to grow things which are either relatively rare or expensive to buy. Vegetables in season are often cheaper to buy in the supermarket than to grow at home, so choose a few crops which are quick to mature and some with a long cropping period, such as courgettes, spinach and the more exotic varieties of lettuce or mixed salad leaves (cut-and-come-again). It's possible to extend your harvest by staggering the times of sowing, ensuring that the crops ripen in succession and you don't end up with a glut of one vegetable.

If the garden is very small, grow herbs, fruit and vegetables in flower borders. Small plants, such as fluffy-headed carrots and leafy lettuces should be placed at the front of the beds, with delicate fronds of fennel and asparagus and the large leaves

of rhubarb behind, and at the back of the border the tallest vegetables such as globe artichokes. Plant peas and beans to scramble up a fence or make a feature of cane wigwams for these and other climbers.

Many herbs, fruit and vegetables are so decorative that it is worth growing them on their own in containers so that their shapes and colours can be fully appreciated. Plant a frilly-leaved lettuce in a pot, or place a colourful miniature pepper plant as a centrepiece to a table. Courgettes are easy to grow and have glorious, trumpet-shaped, yellow blooms.

Be sure to include fruit and vegetables that children can snack on, such as peas – which always taste sweetest when picked straight from the pod – and little cherry tomatoes. Alpine strawberries are also an excellent choice. Plant these as edging to your vegetable beds then send the children off after lunch to pick their pudding. They will be happy for ages, searching for the delicious, succulent little fruit.

While tiny alpine strawberries may escape the full attention of birds it is unlikely that any soft fruit will be so lucky. So if you are planning to grow redcurrants, raspberries or blackcurrants and do not

Above
Fruit, herbs and vegetables will all grow well in containers.

Below
Encourage your child to plant seeds so they can see a plant grow from scratch. Using a transparent container means they can see the roots growing as well.

want to share the fruits of your labours with every bird from miles around then it is worth growing them in a fruit cage. These are simple constructions made of netting and posts which can be bought ready-made then taken down and stored at the end of the growing season. Check carefully from time to time to make sure that there are no tears or gaps in the netting as small birds can easily become trapped inside.

There are many new varieties of fruit that allow gardeners with even very small patches to enjoy picking their own. Look

for dwarf trees and the very slim ballerina breeds. You can maximise space by training trees into fan shapes to grow against the house or as espaliers, cordons or step-overs to work as dividers within the garden.

Like fruit and vegetables, herbs demand a sunny, sheltered spot with well-drained soil. Yet they are happy to grow among the flowers and plants in borders, with fruit and vegetables, alone in a formal herb garden or in pots on the patio.

Herbs are important for more than their flavours. Many have extremely pretty flowers and foliage, are wonderfully aromatic and attract all kinds of insects, especially bees and butterflies (see Chapter 6).

The most basic selection of herbs for the family garden should include rosemary, lavender, mint, parsley, sage and thyme. However, do try to and find space for coriander, oregano and basil, which all look extremely pretty as well as having a delicious fragrance and taste. Mint is very invasive, so if you want to include it in a border or herb garden plant it in a container sunk into the soil, to prevent the roots from spreading.

A formal herb garden adds a special touch to any space and can be quite small. Like European medieval monks, early American settlers grew herbs for medicinal as well as culinary purposes and favoured a simple square or rectangular shape intersected by a path in the shape of a cross and with an island bed in the centre. This may originally have housed a beehive, although nowadays a sundial or obelisk is more practical. Such a design could easily be copied in a space of no more than a few square metres or yards.

In the past herbs have also been used as dyes, and children can have great fun experimenting with these. Most people are familiar with the wonderful blue that comes from indigo, but less well known is that sorrel yields an unusual greeny-yellow dye whilst a good yellow comes from marigolds.

▶dangerous plants

Babies and young children love to put things in their mouths. Young babies, not being very mobile, will happily make do with whatever is immediately to hand. Soil, pebbles, the odd insect, all will be carefully tasted, chewed and then, hopefully, spat out.

Below
Rue is an irritant, so if you find this growing in your garden it is advisable to remove it.

As they get older and more mobile children widen the range of the inedibles they attempt to eat. Anything colourful, especially berries, is tempting, and as many of these are poisonous the potential for disaster is considerable.

Set aside a couple of hours, arm yourself with a list of dangerous plants and take a stroll around your garden. You'll be amazed at the results of your survey. Many of the most commonly grown plants, such as foxgloves and lupins, are poisonous, but do not pose much of a risk as few children would ever be tempted to eat them. It is the plants and trees with berries that pose the problem. Most children cannot distinguish between blackcurrants and deadly night-shade or laburnum seed pods and pea pods, and they are quite likely to think that anything that looks like food must be food.

The first thing to do is to train your children from the earliest age never to put things in their mouths or to eat anything unless you have specifically stated that it is safe. Next remove as many poisonous plants as possible, fence off any others that you want to keep, and make a real effort to remove any berries that fall on the ground.

If you find your child has been eating something poisonous, check that there is not any plant matter left in the mouth, then seek medical advice. Remember to take a sample of the plant with you if you go to the doctor or hospital. Do not try to make the child vomit.

When carrying out your survey of the garden also look out for the many garden plants and weeds that cause skin rashes and allergies. As children tear around a garden they are likely to brush against plants and so fall victim to any irritating leaves, stems or sap.

It is well known that weeds such as poison ivy cause dreadful rashes, yet there are many cultivated plants capable of producing similar if not worse skin reactions. Most dangerous of all are the plants with photo-

sensitive sap, that when exposed to sunlight triggers a chemical reaction which makes the sap incredibly irritating.

Giant hogweed (*Heracleum mantegazzianum*) is a common example of such a plant. It is wonderfully architectural, with its spreading white umbrella flowers on top of tall woody stems. Yet it is best excluded from any garden where children play as there have been numerous cases of children using these hollow woody stems as pea shooters and then developing vicious blisters around their mouths as soon as they go into the sunlight. The blisters can last for weeks, while the underlying damage to the skin may not be repaired for months.

Above
Giant hogweed is a wonderfully architectural plant yet its sap causes vicious blisters.

Right
Monkshood is pretty to look at but dangerous to handle.

common poisonous or irritating plants

Anemone
Autumn crocus
Buttercup
Caster oil plant
Columbine
Daphne
Datura
False acacia
Giant hogweed
Globe flower
Hellebore
Hemlock
Holly
Honeysuckle
Ivy
Kingcup
Laburnum
Larkspur
Laurel
Lily-of-the-valley
Lupin
Monkshood
Morning Glory
Oleander
Poison ivy
Potato (green tubers, leaves and uncooked)
Primula
Privet
Rhubarb
Spindle
Spurge
Stinging nettle
Sumach
Sweet pea
Tomato (stems and leaves)
Yew
• This is not a definitive list.

Above
Caster oil plant can cause skin problems.

Above
Blackthorn shrubs bear sloe berries which make good drinks, but it isn't suitable for a family garden because of its thorns.

Above
Firethorn (*Pyracantha*) has attractive berries and is very hardy but has thorns, so is best situated out of reach from young children.

Other common garden plants which can cause serious skin problems include the spurges (*Euphorbia*), rue (*Ruta* and species), monkshood (*Aconitum* and species), hemlock (*Conium maculatum*), *Colchicum* and species, and the caster oil plant (*Ricinus communis*). Site such plants at the back of the borders where children are less likely to come into contact with them and warn them of the danger.

Plants with spikes and thorns are obviously a danger to children. *Berberis*, *Pyracantha* and sloe (*Prunus spinosa*) all have long, needles, sharp thorns and *Mahonia* and holly leaves are very spiky, especially once they have died and fallen to the ground to dry out. The tips of yucca leaves have especially strong, sharp spikes, and most varieties of roses and blackberries have cruel thorns. However, it would be a shame simply to ban these attractive plants from the garden, so if they cannot be doctored in any way, for example by snipping the tips off the yucca, site them where they are out of the reach of children. Also, clear up old leaves and thorns as they fall.

▶resilient plants

While some plants may pose a danger to children, it is more frequently that children pose a danger (and a deadly one at that) to plants. A vigorous game of football in the wrong place can cause unbelievable destruction.

Below
Geraniums and Lady's Mantle are great plants that will grow quickly and will survive the odd mishap.

To avoid living in a constant state of anxiety about the damage that is being wrought to plants every time the children go out to play, design your garden so that the planting around the children's main play area comprises only the most hardy, vigorous and forgiving plants and shrubs. Anything at all delicate must be moved to another part of the garden, where it can thrive in peace.

If you have grass, be sure that it is a hardy variety and do not cut it lower than 1.2-2.5cm/1/2-1in. Grow perennials low and medium height that will happily regenerate themselves. Geraniums are particularly useful as they spread freely and are so hardy that they can easily cope with the occasional trampling. Similarly the ivies (*Hedera*) are extremely tough and recover quickly from being crushed and having strands ripped off to make into crowns or garlands.

Some flowers such as foxgloves (*Digitalis*) and poppies (*Papaver*), actually benefit from being brushed against and having the ground around them disturbed, as this helps to spread their seeds over a wider area. Lady's mantle (*Alchemilla mollis*) is also a prodigious self-seeder that will quickly make up for any damage it sustains.

Of the shrubs, buddleia is virtually indestructible and will soon recover even after whole branches have been ripped off. *Viburnum* and *Euonymus* also cope well with rough treatment and mallows (*Lavatera*) will continue to produce their wonderful stems of hollyhock-like flowers almost as fast as children can pick them.

Privet (*Ligustrum*) is another useful shrub in several ways. Besides being extremely tough, it makes a good dense hedge and can be cut into all manner of shapes if you want to experiment with topiary. As an unusual bonus its cuttings can be used to feed any stick insects the children may be keeping as pets.

▶low maintenance gardening

For many families, especially those with very young children, life is a constant race against time. Apart from work, school and socialising there may be ballet, swimming, football and all manner of other extra-curricular activities to be fitted into the day.

Right
A busy family life leaves little time for gardening, but if you make it a family activity, it will seem less of a chore.

The fact is that many of us simply do not have the time to spend lavishing attention on the garden.

If this sounds like your problem there are numerous things you can do to minimise the need for constant maintenance, yet still have an attractive garden.

Aim for an uncomplicated natural layout, as anything too formal demands a great deal of attention to keep it looking trim. Avoid annual bedding plants, that need to be dug up at the end of each season and instead choose plants that will take care of themselves.

Bulbs and perennials appear year after year and, despite admonishments in many gardening books that they should be lifted and divided after blooming, will happily repeat their display with virtually no attention at all.

Better still, numerous plants, such as anemone, dead nettle (*Lamium*), periwinkle (*Vincas*) and geranium, provide vital ground covers spreading vigorously without any human assistance and smother weeds while looking good.

Other tips are to choose shrubs, especially evergreens, which naturally grow into an attractive shape and eliminate the need to spend hours clipping and training. Plant climbers that are self-clinging rather than twining, so that you do not need put up trellis or wires then tie them in.

Lawns are relatively high maintenance areas because they require regular mowing, but the open space is very useful in a family garden. Instead of converting your lawn to paving or gravel, set a brick or paving surround flush with the soil surface and the mower will be able to cut right to the edge, so avoiding the back-breaking chore of edging with shears.

Containers look lovely, but keep them to a minimum as they are labour intensive requiring constant watering in dry weather and re-potting at the start of each season.

Soft fruit and vegetables also require a lot of attention, so don't be too ambitious until the children are old enough not to pose a risk to containers and plants. Consider installing an automatic watering system (see chapter three). These are invaluable for anyone who does not have much time to spend on the garden.

recycling

How green is your garden? A garden gives ample scope to indulge green tendencies in more ways than one. Gardeners who cannot be bothered to recycle organic waste, whether it be dead plant matter or household items, ignore a valuable resource. They both deprive their garden of nourishing food and create more work for themselves in the process.

▶ compost

Compost is a dark, rich, sweet-smelling, crumbly substance which improves soil condition by adding water-retaining humus and nitrogen – vital for the wellbeing of plants.

Above
Set aside a corner of the garden for a compost heap. All kinds of natural waste from tea bags to chopped grass can be composted and recycled into the garden.

Compost can be bought, but is so easy to make that there is little excuse for not producing your own. There is a two-fold advantage to making compost. First you are creating something for free which will improve the garden immeasurably, second you know you are making good use of your waste and not taking up valuable space in a landfill site. Dig the compost into your soil, or spread it over the surface when the soil is damp, to act as a mulch.

Virtually any organic material can be composted. From the house collect tea bags, vegetable peelings, eggshells, shredded newspaper, even old cotton or woollen rags. And from the garden save waste such as dead flowers and leaves, bolted vegetables and old bedding plants, grass clippings, soft prunings, hedge trimmings and weeds

(before they have set seed). Even the children can help by collecting their pet's droppings when they clean out their cages. These will heat things up splendidly, speeding the process of decomposition.

Do not use meat, any cooked food, or anything greasy as this will attract vermin. Discard and burn any parts of diseased plants, seed-bearing annual weeds, or the roots of perennial weeds, such as ground elder (*Aegopodium podagraria*) and couch grass (*Agropyron repens*). These are so tough that they can survive the composting process and you will end up spreading your problems. Anything too woody will not decompose, so either use a shredder or burn such material.

If space allows, have two heaps or bins. This will ensure a constant supply of compost, as material can be rotting down in one bin while you are still filling the other.

traditional compost heaps

There are numerous methods of making compost. Compost heaps suit large gardens that produce masses of waste. However, completely open heaps are unsightly and inefficient, so it is better to buy, or make an enclosure. Do-it-yourself containers can be put together from wooden pallets and wire or you can buy kits which, when assembled, form brick and wood bins, or slatted timber enclosures.

With open heaps such as these the material at the edges, where it is cooler, will not compost at the same rate as that in the middle, so the heap will need to be turned regularly. To this end, do not overfill the bin. You could tip it out to mix. Cover it with a sheet of polythene or old carpet to keep off heavy rain, but don't allow it to dry out in summer. To ensure there is enough material to heat up sufficiently, the heap or bin must be a minimum of 90cm/ 3ft square by 1.2m/4ft high.

Above
You can disguise your compost bin by making or buying a cover. One with slats will allow air to circulate.

Above
Use natural kitchen waste in your compost, such as peelings, eggshells and shredded newspaper but don't add greasy food or meat.

ready-made compost bins

If you do not want to make a compost enclosure yourself, there are numerous ready-made plastic and metal bins on the market. These are usually fully enclosed, which means that the composted material will heat up evenly and rot down quickly, eliminating the tedious job of turning the compost. The bins are also designed for ease of access to the composted material at the bottom.

wormeries

These differ from ready-made compost bins in that they rely on a colony of worms (tiger or brandling worms) to produce the compost. The worms are put in specially-designed worm bins on a layer of material which has already rotted down. They are then given fresh supplies of finely chopped household scraps every few days. The bins have a tray to collect liquid, which can be drained off, diluted with water then used for plant food. The resulting compost is wonderfully rich. There are disadvantages to this system however. Wormeries are not easy to get going, the worms need regular supplies and they must be sieved out when the bin is full and it is time to start a new one – not a pleasant task.

leaf mould

The fallen leaves of deciduous trees, especially oak, beech and elm, make wonderful compost. Pile large amounts in a corner or leaf bin. This is basically a wire cage, and is very simple to make from a roll of chicken wire and four wooden posts. Put smaller amounts in black plastic sacks, seal them and punch some holes in the sides. The leaves will take about a year to compost down although you can speed up the process by shredding them and using a leaf compost activator.

making compost

• Start with a thick base of rough, bulky material, such as straw or shredded prunings, then sprinkle with either sulphate of ammonia (a dessertspoon per square metre/yard), or a bought compost activator or fresh animal manure, to speed up decomposition.
• Continue building up the heap in 15cm/6in layers, adding a little lime to alternate layers if you wish. Avoid adding too much of any one thing at a time, for example too many grass clippings will result in a smelly, black slime rather then the sweet, crumbling consistency formed by successful composting.

green compost

An attractive alternative to traditional compost is green compost. This process uses living plants, which are grown solely to be dug back into the soil to condition it. Green compost works well for light sandy, or heavy clay soils and has the bonus of demanding less effort than collecting, turning and spreading home-made compost. Sow the crop to be composted in late summer, cut it just as it flowers in early spring, and allow it to lie for a few days. Then dig it in and leave for a couple of months before planting something else.

Excellent plants for fixing nitrogen in the soil are alsike clover (*Trifolium hybridum*) and lupins (*Lupinus*), but borage (*Borago officinalis*), mustard (*Brassica rapa* or *B. nigra*) and comfrey (*Symphytum officinale*) also make excellent green manures.

One obvious disadvantage of this method is that the soil cannot be used for any other plants while the cover crop is growing. However if you choose a pretty enough green manure this need not be a problem.

▶inorganic recycling

Below
Construct a drip-watering system using old plastic bottles and rubber tubes.

Most families generate a quite shocking amount of waste. Luckily, with a bit of imagination, many things can be given a second lease of life.

Holed kettles can be pushed sideways into a hedge for small birds to nest in, a chipped mug can be hung up as a birdfeeder, old carpets can be used on top of the compost heap to help all the ingredients heat up, and plastic photographic film containers are perfect for storing seeds.

Polystyrene packaging makes an excellent alternative to crocks as drainage material for containers. In fact, if you are planting up containers for a balcony or roof garden, polystyrene is really ideal as it is so

light it reduces the weight of the containers.

Virtually anything that can hold water can be used as a plant container, from ancient wellington boots to old tin baths, plastic buckets and ancient cracked butler's sinks. Be careful not to over-clutter your garden, however. It's best to tuck these items away in foliage, so that you come to them as a surprise.

artificial mulches

Pieces of old carpet, thick layers of news-paper, plastic fertiliser bags and sheets of cardboard can all be used to clear an area of obstinate weeds. Just cover the ground and leave it alone for a year. As the soil is deprived of light nothing will be able to grow and all the troublesome weeds will die. Disguise your mulching material with gravel or bark if it looks too ugly.

water features

Washing-up bowls, old baking trays, upturned dustbin lids and pans are all excellent candidates for transformation into miniature water features. They can either be left unplanted as informal bird baths, or

making a scarecrow

A scarecrow will not only keep the birds from doing damage to the gar-den but will provide an amusing focal point and a fun project for the chil-dren. If it is moved every once in a while and perhaps given a change of clothes the birds will not have a chance to get used to it.

1 Use an old broom handle or mop as the upright and a thick garden cane as the horizontal. Make a frame by lashing together some hazel canes in a tall cross shape.

2 The head can be a swede or cab-bage topped with an old hat or you could use a mop head.

3 Clothe the scarecrow in an old shirt or jacket and pair of trousers, and finish off with a scarf, or you could make a lady scarecrow.

As an additional bird-scaring device give your scarecrow some tin-foil streamers or maybe a mirror to hold, to reflect the sun's rays.

Above

Almost anything can be used as a container for plants. Add a few holes for drainage, and plant as normal!

can be planted up to form perfect small-scale habitats that will attract a surprising number of wild visitors. Don't forget to keep the water very shallow if you have small children.

watering systems

A cheap way to install automatic watering is to make your own discreet watering device out of an old plastic drinks bottle.

1) Cut out a hole in the base of the bottle, just large enough to be able to water through.

2) Loosen the cap of the bottle then place it upside down in the pot so the base of the bottle slightly pokes just above the surface of the compost.

3) Fill the bottle with water through the hole in the base and it will slowly seep out of the loosened cap, providing your thirsty plants with just the correct amount of water that they need.

An alternative is to cut an old plastic drinks bottle in half. Make three or four small holes in the base, then stick it in a grow-bag of, for example, tomatoes (being very thirsty plants). Fill the half-bottle with water and it will slowly trickle through the holes to ensure the tomatoes never dry out.

It is also possible to buy specially made spikes which fit on the top of a two-litre plastic drinks bottle. Once the bottle is inverted you can stick the spikes into the ground and their ingenious little holes release water or liquid nutrients slowly. As the spike penetrates so far into the ground the water or feed will be at the right level to reach the roots.

a lacewing home

The larvae of lacewings are a gardener's true friends, as they prey on aphids. To boost your garden's lacewing population create a comfortable place for them to breed. Take an old, plastic, soft drinks bottle and cut off the base. Now roll up a sheet of corrugated paper and insert it into the bottomless bottle, securing it with large paper clips or wire. Hang it up in a tree for the winter and the lacewings should lay eggs in it.

home-made cloches

Glass cloches are now classified as antiques and so have accordingly high price tags. You might be lucky enough to find some at second-hand shops or car-boot sales, so keep an eye out. There are cheaper plastic alternatives available, but if you need to cover a whole row of plants these will also work out rather expensive. An alternative is to use jam jars for emerging shoots, then as they get larger, slice the bottoms off plastic bottles and use these as cloches for the small young plants. Leafy vegetables prone to slug and snail attack, such as lettuce, will especially benefit from this protection. Discard the lids as the plants need fresh air.

planters

Yoghurt cartons, jam jars and the bottom halves of drinks bottles are perfect containers for seedlings. Jam jars have the advantage of weight, making them less likely to blow over than lighter plastic items. But as it is impossible to make a hole in the bottom of the jar safely be sure to half-fill it with gravel or small pebbles for drainage.

You and your children could decorate your home-made planters by painting them with a matt acrylic paint or by sticking on shells, twigs or pieces of broken china.

home-made cobbles

Use empty yoghurt cartons as moulds to make your own cobbles. Simply mix up some concrete then pour into the cartons. Allow to set then tap out the finished cobble. Special powder dyes can be added to the concrete when it is being mixed to change its colour.

Above
An earthenware jug makes a good resting place for a bird, and is also a good place for bird food.

Left
A cluster of homemade cloches made out of old plastic bottles work like mini greenhouses.

dangers

The number of children who are seriously injured in the garden every year is staggering. In the UK alone the figure is more than 125,000 and the number of minor accidents is unquantifiable, as few ever get reported. Most of these injuries would never have happened if a few simple precautions had only been taken.

▶general dangers

Above
Attach chicken wire over potentially slippery areas such as wood and stone.

There are many dangers in a garden, but there are precautions you can take:

• Firstly be disciplined when you garden. Lock away all tools and chemicals. Accidents with gardening tools, both manual and electrical, account for 100,000 injuries to children every year in the UK. Garden chemicals can be very dangerous and include weedkillers, pesticides, fertilisers, fungicides, disinfectants and petrol.

• Don't store chemicals anywhere that gets very hot, such as a greenhouse, as they may give off poisonous fumes or even catch fire. Keep oil and petrol in metal containers and if possible buy chemicals that have had a bittering agent added. This makes them unpalatable if a child does manage to get hold of them. Don't store chemicals in old soft drinks bottles.

• Keep children away from any area which has been treated recently with weedkiller, pesticide or fertiliser – even if the packet says it is child friendly.

• Watch out for uneven surfaces which could trip up children or elderly people. Maintain all paths and steps, replacing broken paving slabs, steps and loose stones.

• Prevent paths, steps and patios becoming slippery by removing any overhanging branches. These encourage moss and algae to grow in their shade. Scrub off the algae and moss with hot soapy water or spray it with a high-pressure water jet attached to your hose pipes. This is preferable to using chemical cleaners that may damage the hard surface in time. Sprinkling sharp sand over problem areas helps to provide grip and rub off algae. Wooden steps become very slippery once wet, so fit chicken wire. Occasional use of a stiff brush also prevents green slime coating timber surfaces such as old railway sleepers.

• Look out for protruding stems or branches beside paths which may scratch or cause eye injuries. Buy rubber cane tops for all cane plant supports.

• Your garden design should never include unprotected sharp drops. Those from a patio are especially dangerous, as running or cycling children can go over the edge. Site greenhouses carefully where children are safe from the danger of broken glass and the greenhouse is safe from flying footballs.

• Never site play equipment near a greenhouse, railings, cold frame or washing line.

• All gates should be fitted with childproof locks and it's best to avoid fences with horizontal rails because children can climb them. Be as prompt as possible in mending holes in hedges and fences as children can squeeze through the smallest gaps.

▶burning refuse

Children find fire irresistible. Whether it is a small fire in a brazier or a fully fledged blazing bonfire, the smell of smoke and the glow and crackle of the flames will attract them as surely as wasps to jam.

Autumn is the best time for bonfires. Choose a windless day, so the fire is safe to control and you won't have to dodge the plumes of smoke as they constantly change direction. Before you light the fire check for any small mammals, such as hedgehogs, which may have crawled into the pile to shelter or hibernate. In spring make sure

The first rule is never to leave unattended any fire in the garden, even if it is only a barbecue. Bonfires should be built away from sheds, fences, plants and overhanging branches. Consider your neighbour and don't position or light a bonfire if the smoke is likely to blow towards their house or garden.

Keep your bonfire material dry so that it will burn quickly without producing clouds of choking smoke. You can cover the pile with a sheet of plastic or tarpaulin until you are ready to burn.

there are no birds' nests being built. Place a few buckets of water nearby in case of emergencies. Try not to breathe in smoke as some plants give off poisonous fumes and be wary of any stones or even bits of glass, which may explode in the heat.

Instead of banning children from the garden when you are having a bonfire, set them small tasks, for example scouring the garden for waste material to burn or being on fire bucket duty. They will be kept busy, have lots of fun, and will feel involved so will be far less likely to get up to mischief.

▶water safety

Drowning in ponds and paddling pools accounts for the highest number of deaths among children in the garden. It is a terrifying fact that babies and small children can drown in as little as 5 cm/2in of water.

Below
Place a strong fence around an existing pool prevents danger to young children.

Older children and adults automatically hold their breath when their head goes under water, but small children and babies do exactly the opposite and take a deep breath in order to scream. Instead of getting a lungful of air, they get a lungful of water, and so drown.

So be aware that if you have water in your garden it is potentially a fatal hazard. Some water features, such as small ponds and pools, can be filled in, eliminating the risk altogether. This is not practical or even possible for large ponds, swimming pools or streams, in which case you must take precautions to reduce the danger.

Once drained a shallow pond may be turned into a sunken herb garden or sandpit which will need a lid to stop it being flooded by rain. Larger ponds make excellent play areas once they are drained and filled with bark, wood chippings or sand.

If you do not want to drain your pool, cover it with rigid wire mesh. There are many makes on the market which are robust enough to take the weight of a child. Many are coloured green to be unobtrusive and large aquatic plants will grow through the holes in the mesh.

Swimming pools should be fitted with strong, child-proof covers and fenced off. Put a child-resistant lock on the gate and never leave children unsupervised in the pool, even if they are able to swim. Don't allow unsupervised play in a paddling pool either and when the children have finished playing, empty it and turn it upside down to prevent it filling up with rainwater.

Gardens in a river-side setting are extremely desirable, but risks to children are obvious. The only solution is to erect a stout fence. This need not be an eyesore as you can disguise it by growing shrubs and flowers in front of it or planting climbers which can be trained up and along it. In this way it becomes an attractive feature until the children are old enough for it to be taken down.

▶plant pests and diseases

Pests and diseases are killers for plants and need to be kept at bay. Pest and disease control falls into two categories: prevention and cure.

prevention

Firstly buy only the choicest plant specimens. Choose the most healthy, vigorous-looking plants and check that their roots are not pot-bound, and that the plant is not dried out or already harbouring some pest or disease. You can often tell if a plant has been too long in its container as there is moss growing on the surface of the compost. Check also that you are not inadvertently buying some weeds along with your plant – the last thing anyone wants to do is to introduce yet another problem into the garden. Certain plants have been bred with disease-resistant varieties. Seek these out wherever possible as it will save a lot of trouble later on, especially if you are growing roses.

Follow the recommendations as to planting position and conditions exactly, for if you place a plant in an unsuitable position it will not thrive, no matter how healthy it is initially, or however much love, care and attention you lavish on it.

Practice good husbandry. Clear away weeds and debris which could provide hiding places for pests or act as a breeding ground for disease. Remove any dead, damaged or diseased parts of plants, and always burn such material. Clean out the greenhouse regularly and be meticulous about cleaning and disinfecting your tools, especially secateurs, shears and pots to prevent the spread of infection.

Erect barriers to deter pests. For example net vegetables and grow soft fruit in a simple cage to keep the birds away. Protect fruit trees from pests by putting a grease band around the trunk in winter.

Spread gravel, prickly holly leaves or soot around the base of vulnerable plants, or, if they are grown in pots, paint pest-control glue around the rims. Slugs and snails cannot bear to cross such protective barriers and gravel has the added advantage of acting as an excellent mulch.

cure

If you still have a problem there are numerous methods of controlling pests and diseases. However, do remember that the safest way is the organic way.

manual pest removal

This is the most basic method of pest control and can be rather tedious work, however it is also extremely satisfying – some even say addictive. Picking off pests,

Above

A ladybird is one bug you should try to keep in your garden. Ladybirds are not only pretty but they also eat unwanted pests.

such as caterpillars, by hand (if you are squeamish, wear thin gloves for this operation). Don't just throw them away in a corner of the garden, as they'll simply return. They must be destroyed, for effective control. You will need to repeat the procedure at intervals of one or two weeks, until there are no signs of further infestation.

An effective way of dealing with slugs and snails is to go out with a torch and a bucket of soapy water at night, pick off the slugs and snails then drop them in the bucket. This, however, is not a job for the faint-hearted. If you want to give slugs and snails a happy death, place bowls of beer stuck into the ground among your flowerbeds.

Sticky insect traps have been used in greenhouses for a hundred years or so and work just as well today. Position the traps very close to the plants under attack and brush the plants to encourage the insects to leave them.

Set earwig traps by filling a flowerpot with straw or crumpled newspaper, then placing it upside down on a cane in the flowerbed. Check it daily and remove and destroy any earwigs you find.

You can wash aphids off plants with repeated sprayings of soapy water but remember that birds, hoverflies and ladybirds adore eating them. In fact one ladybird can apparently dispose of a massive 500 aphid larva and 5000 adults during its lifetime.

companion planting

Certain plants, especially vegetables, benefit from companion planting, the growing of one plant beside another specifically to deter pests, distract them from the main plant, or attract their predators. Strong-smelling herbs, such as mint, are excellent for this job.

Most people are aware that French marigolds (*Tagetes patula*) attract hoverflies, which love to eat aphids, therefore it makes sense to grow them beside any vegetable, that is susceptible to aphid attack.

Rosemary and lavender are dried and used as a deterrent to stop moths from attacking linen and clothes, and grown in the garden these herbs protect plants from caterpillar attack. Moths also hate the strong smell of wormwood (*Artemesia absinthium*), which can be grown as a companion plant, or made into an infusion to spray plants in need of protection.

As a preventative against diseases, horsetail is a herb which works as a natural fungicide. It is effective against blackspot and mildew on roses.

natural predators

Avoid the necessity of chemical controls by encouraging beneficial predators. Learn to distinguish the goodies from the baddies, for example centipedes are good, millipedes are bad; carnivorous beetles are good, herbivorous beetles are bad. Once you have identified friends and foes you can start to encourage beneficial predators by avoiding chemicals and creating a habitat that your insect and animal helpers can enjoy (see Chapter 6).

Insect-eating birds such as blue tits, are very welcome, as are ladybirds. Encourage these natural predators by filling a box with hollow stems from dead herbaceous plants and fixing it high up a tree, or on a wall where they can hibernate. You also want

Right
Small insects roll up when threatened. They are not harmful to children unless a child attempts to eat one.

plenty of spiders, hoverflies, lacewing larvae, centipedes, carnivorous beetles, frogs, toads, shrews and hedgehogs – which can eat an amazing two hundred slugs a night.

biological control

This is a relatively new method of pest control but one which can be extremely effective, if somewhat expensive. It involves the introduction of microscopic parasitic insects, that feed off the pest and ultimately kill it. Examples are *Phytoseiulus*, which targets red spider mites or *Encarsia formosa*, a parasitic wasp which attacks whitefly. However, such controls tend to work best in enclosed areas such as greenhouses and conservatories. If a plant has previously been sprayed with any kind of chemical, the eggs of the parasitic insect may fail to hatch.

Many garden centres and mail order companies supply biological controls and they are easy to apply. Nematodes, for example, are microscopic, parasitic eelworms used to treat slugs and vine weevils. They are made up into a solution, then watered into the soil around the affected plants. It is, however, important to follow the supplier's instructions as to application times. If you release them when it is too cold they will die. They will also die soon after their victims are destroyed, as there will be nothing for them to feed off so you will need to replace them the following year or until the problem is eradicated.

chemical control

Chemicals should only be used as a last resort. If there is no alternative it is essential to use them responsibly and sparingly so that you affect beneficial wildlife as little as possible. For example, if you have tried unsuccessfully every other way of controlling snails and slugs and feel slug pellets are the only remaining option, you should use the following method

Make a slit down one side of a plastic water bottle and bend the edges back. Scatter pellets inside and half bury the bottle among the plants under attack. The slugs and snails will crawl into the bottle, eat the pellets and die. Ensure the pesticides are out of reach of small children, who may think the brightly coloured pellets are sweets. The pellets should be also kept away from the soil so they cannot contaminate it. The bodies of the slugs and snails, which are now full of pesticide, are contained in the bottle to be disposed of safely where birds or other predators cannot reach them.

When spraying chemicals, ensure that all pets and children are kept well away from the area – even if the label says the chemicals will not harm them. To avoid harming beneficial insects spray on a dull and windless day – they will be less active than on a hot sunny one. If you have pond fish, make sure there is absolutely no spray drift over the water, as fish are extremely sensitive to any contact with chemicals.

Wear protective clothing, including goggles and gloves and wash away immediately any accidental splashes on bare skin using lots of cold water.

Keep separate watering cans and spray guns that are reserved solely for chemical use and label them so there is no risk of confusion.

Other pests which are easily treatable by this method include whitefly, red spider mite, leatherjackets and scale insects.

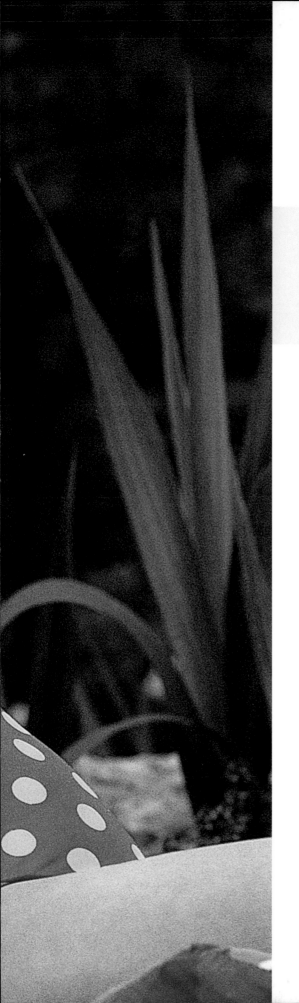

first aid and childcare

In the event of any accident the first thing to do is to stay calm. Your child is dependent upon you for help, so you must be able to think calmly and clearly.

If a child is lying injured, call for an ambulance at once. However, do not replace the telephone on the receiver – even if you have had to dash back to the child before speaking to the operator. If you have not been able to give your full address and telephone number but you leave the line open, the emergency services can trace your address and send aid. They can also give you instructions over the phone and help you stay calm.

Take the child to hospital if they have fallen uncon-scious (even for a moment), are vomiting or drowsy (as there is a risk of concussion or shock), are bleeding from the ears or have stopped breathing (even for a moment). Hospital treatment is also required if the child has a puncture wound, or com-plains of severe pain.

Do make sure all your family's tetanus injections are kept up-to-date and it's wise to sign yourself up for a proper first aid course to give you greater con-fidence with your first aid skills.

▸sun protection

The sun is a powerful life-giving force, without which no life on the planet would be possible. However, we now know that its power can be destructive. In the UK alone there are more than 40,000 new cases of skin cancer diagnosed every year, of which about 2,000 are untreatable. In the US skin cancer is the biggest cause of death among women of 25 and 30 years old. Treatment for skin cancer is unpleasant and leaves the patient with scars.

Above
The sun beating down on a child's head can cause sunstroke, so it is important to ensure that a hat is worn at all times, so your child can enjoy their time in the sun.

Even people who know how dangerous the sun can be, find it difficult to shake off the idea that an attractive tan makes you feel good and unhealthy. But the skin turns brown in an attempt to protect itself from harmful rays, so a tan is a visible indication of damaged skin. Although it may look good in the short term, a tan soon fades, while the damage caused to the skin is permanent and can cause premature ageing. Wrinkled, leathery skin is a legacy of excessive sun worship and inadequate precautions while young.

The effects of too much sun are also cumulative and our children will not thank us in years to come if we don't protect them when they are at a vulnerable age. Babies and children, especially blonde, blue-eyed children from the northern hemisphere, have very delicate, sensitive skin which burns easily, even in sunlight too weak to affect grown-ups.

However it is unrealistic and unreasonable to expect them to stay in the shade when it is sunny so it is vital to screen harmful rays.

Most children delight in wearing bright, colourful T-shirts, even in swimming or paddling pools. There are also wonderful ultraviolet-proof all-in-one suits, which look just like wet-suits so have a great cool cachet for even the most obstinate child.

Heads, faces and backs of necks are very vulnerable, so hats are important. For younger children there are French Legionnaire-style hats to protect the back of the neck and ears – areas often forgotten when sunscreens are applied. Older children can be quite difficult about wearing hats. Girls may be persuaded if they are allowed to choose their own creation but boys can be a bit more tricky. A baseball cap in the colours of their favourite sports

Right
Encourage your child
to apply sun block and
to rest in the shade.

team, or personalised cap with fabric paints might work. The only disadvantage of baseball caps is that they don't cover the ears or the neck, unless worn back to front so don't dispense with the sun protection cream.

Choose a sun protection cream of factor 20 or above, apply it generously an hour before the child goes out, then every hour or so while the child is in the sun and especially after swimming. Try to avoid being in full sun during the hottest part of the day, and have lunch in the shade. If swimming is the afternoon activity make sure that lunch is fully digested before your child takes the plunge.

Harmful rays penetrate cloud and even burn when the sky is overcast. Water intensifies rays, so if you have a swimming or paddling pool apply extra cream.

Never leave a baby sleeping in the sun but always use a sunshade and check the baby frequently as the sun moves around.

If your child does get burnt gently cool the red areas with cold tap water and apply calamine lotion or an after-sun lotion to

soothe the skin. Bring the child indoors so they can rest and recover out of the sun. Take the child to the doctor if there is blistering of the skin over a wide area, or if the child develops a fever (a possible sign of sunstroke).

Make sure your child has plenty to drink on a sunny day so they keep cool and hydrated.

Below
Remember to reapply
sun block throughout
the day.

▶minor injuries

While minor sunburn, stings, bites, cuts, grazes, thorns and splinters can be treated at home, more serious injuries require hospital attention and the first aid techniques described in this chapter are no more than emergency measures. If you have any doubt or unease whatsoever as to the seriousness of your child's injury, call your local hospital or doctor's surgery and explain the situation.

Below
Knee and elbow pads and helmets will help protect against any nasty falls from bicycles, skateboards and rollerskates.

cuts and grazes

Most children go through a stage when they seem constantly to be falling over and cutting or grazing themselves. This is when a well-stocked first aid box is invaluable. Knees and elbows take the most punishment but you can take preventative action. For example, persuade your child to wear elbow and knee protectors when skating or cycling and buy them good, thick trousers to wear when they are climbing.

Cuts and grazes can usually be treated at home. Common sense should tell you if a child needs medical attention, for example if the cut is especially large or deep, if something is embedded in it, or it is too dirty to clean easily.

Clean cuts or grazes either with cold running water, cotton wool soaked in warm water, or antiseptic wipes. Once it is thoroughly clean a graze can be left uncovered to heal, whereas cuts should be protected and kept clean with a plaster or dressing. Change this every day until the cut has healed. Check for any signs of infection such as inflammation, soreness, or tenderness on the area of the cut.

If the cut is still bleeding after five minutes, make a pad using a piece of clean fabric such as a handkerchief – and press it against the wound for a few minutes. If possible raise the limb with the cut above the level of the child's heart to stop the bleeding. Never use a tourniquet.

thorns and splinters

Children act as magnets for all sorts of thorns and splinters, a state of affairs not helped by their sometimes steadfast refusal to wear shoes in the garden.

Holly, mahonia, pyracantha and berberis are just a few of a long list of shrubs and plants with spikes and thorns which can be found in most gardens. It is inevitable that your child will manage to get a thorn or splinter embedded in their hand or foot at some point – possibly every day of the summer holidays if you are unlucky.

A very small thorn or splinter might not hurt and if left alone may pop out of its own accord, often in a warm bath. If, however, it is large or in the heel or fingertips it is bound to be painful and will need to be removed. The hardest part will probably be keeping the child still. Try to get them interested in what you are doing, or tell them a story to distract and calm them.

If you can see the tip of the splinter use a pair of tweezers that you have sterilised in a flame and cooled, you should be able gently to pull it out. Pull it out straight to avoid breaking it, then wash the skin thoroughly and dab on a drop of antiseptic.

If the tip of the splinter is just below the skin, you will need to sterilise a needle (again in a flame) and when it is cool use it to break the skin above the embedded tip of the splinter. Once the tip is revealed, use the needle point to lift it up enough to grasp it with the sterilised tweezers and pull out. Again, clean the area and dab on some antiseptic.

Slivers of glass, metal or painfully large splinters will need medical attention. Watch out for signs of infection, such as swelling, reddening or undue tenderness.

bites, stings and allergic reactions

Whether at home or on holiday, the majority of bites and stings children are likely to suffer will only be minor, and although they may be painful they will not be dangerous. However, there is always a possibility that the child will develop an allergic reaction to a sting which could bring on a convulsion, or in the worst case, anaphylactic shock. This is a life-threatening condition and you must get the child straight to hospital.

Major bites and stings, from spiders, snakes or scorpions, are very dangerous and require urgent hospital treatment. Even if the child appears to show no ill effects, symptoms may develop later.

It may not be possible to identify the source of the wound, but if you can identify or describe the creature responsible, it will help the doctor to provide the right antidote. The first thing to do is to keep the child calm and sit them down, keeping the wound lower than the child's heart if possible. This slows down the spread of the poison. Don't attempt to suck the poison out, but wash around the area and take the child straight to hospital. If the child slips into unconsciousness, check their breathing and begin artificial respiration if it has stopped. If they are still breathing, place them in the recovery position and call an ambulance.

Treatment for minor stings is straight forward. If the sting is from a bee, it will be left embedded in the skin and should be removed carefully. Wasps remove their sting and may therefore sting more than once. Place a clean cloth soaked in very cold water over the wound. The skin around it will soon swell becoming itchy and red, so soothe it with some calamine lotion, then apply some antihistamine ointment.

Occasionally children are stung in the mouth, in which case a cold drink will help reduce the swelling. Sucking an ice cube may also help, but do not give one to a child under two because of the danger of choking.

Certain plants can trigger an allergic reaction in children (see Chapter 7).

Above
Overhanging branches could be dangerous so keep trimmed.

Above
Look out for thorns, although once experienced, most children will stay away!

Above
Berries may look tempting to a child, but many will cause a stomach upset.

▶emergency action

Below
It is vital that every parent knows how to place someone in the recovery position. It makes recovery from trauma easier and is more comfortable for the patient.

However careful you are, accidents can still happen, because children are so active and unpredictable. If there is a bad accident and the child is unconscious there are a few basic emergency rules which may make the difference between life and death.

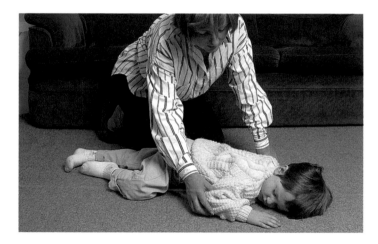

On finding a child unconscious, your first reaction will probably be to rush straight over to help them, but you should take a second to assess the situation in case there maybe some danger which might incapacitate or hinder your rescue attempt. Check for danger: you will not be able to provide much help if you also have an accident.

Now check the child's responses. Talk to them, call their name, tap the soles of their feet, but never shake them, as this could worsen any injury.

If there is no response, the child is unconscious and you must check their breathing immediately as any delay in getting air into

their lungs may result in brain damage. Place your head sideways so you have one ear by the child's mouth and nose and you are looking down at the chest. This way you can listen for breathing, feel any breath against your cheek and look down at the chest to see if it is moving. Allow 10 seconds for this.

If you cannot detect any breathing you must give mouth-to-mouth resuscitation (also known as artificial respiration or mouth-to-mouth ventilation).

First make sure that nothing is blocking the child's airway. Open the mouth and using your finger gently clear away any obvious obstruction which may be preventing the child from breathing, such as vomit or dirt. Do this very carefully to avoid pushing any obstruction further down their throat. Now roll the child on to their back and tilt their head back by lifting the chin with one hand and gently pressing their forehead with your other hand. Open the child's mouth. This movement will lift the tongue away from the back of their throat.

mouth-to-mouth resuscitation

Resuscitation techniques are different for babies and children under two, compared with older children.

Tilt the baby's or toddler's head back and place one hand on their forehead and the other under the back of the neck to support the head in the correct position. Now breathe into the mouth and nose simultaneously.

For older children with one hand pinch the child's nostrils together, place your other hand on their chin to hold the mouth open, then put your mouth completely over the child's and blow gently until you see their chest rise. Stop blowing and allow the chest to fall then repeat the action four times. If after five breaths the child is still not breathing, check their circulation by listening for a heartbeat or feeling for a pulse. The carotid pulse in the neck is the easiest to find by placing two fingers in the hollows on either side of the voice box. Allow 10 seconds to detect the pulse.

If there is no pulse you must give chest compressions (also known as heart massage) as well as mouth-to-mouth resuscitation. Ask someone to help if available.

chest compressions

Place the heel of your hand just above the V where the ribs meet the breastbone and press down to a third of the depth of the chest five times, taking 5 seconds to complete the cycle. For babies and children under two, use only two fingers and exert less pressure to avoid damaging the ribs.

Now alternate the mouth-to-mouth resuscitation and chest compressions at a rate of one breath to five compressions. If the child has a pulse, but is not breathing, administer 10 breaths a minute, then check the pulse for 10 seconds. Once the heart starts beating stop the compressions, but continue artificial respiration until the child or baby starts breathing unaided.

An easy way to remember the routine is to think of it as **ABC**. **A** is for airways, **B** is for breathing, **C** is for circulation. All must be checked, and assisted in that order.

recovery position

Once the child has a pulse and is able to breathe on their own, place them in the recovery position. If someone is left lying on their back while unconscious there is a danger that they may choke on their tongue or vomit. The recovery position prevents the tongue from obstructing the passage of air, unless you think they may have a broken back or neck.

Roll the child gently on to their side, then straighten the lower leg, bend the top leg, stretch out the lower arm, then bend the top arm and rest the head on it. This will prevent them from rolling onto their back.

shock and concussion

After a bad accident a child may well suffer shock. This is potentially a life-threatening state of collapse which must be taken seriously. It is the body's way of coping with an injury, by drawing blood away from the extremities towards the vital organs.

There are various symptoms of shock. The child may seem drowsy or confused, their breathing may become quite shallow and fast, and their skin cold, pale and sweaty. The skin under the fingernails or inside their lips may take on a grey-blue tinge and they may even lose consciousness.

Call an ambulance, then place the child on their back. As long as you are sure there is no head or leg injury, raise their legs 20cm/8in to help more blood go to the head. Place a cushion or pillow beneath the feet to keep them raised and cover the child with a blanket. Do not, however, allow them to get too hot.

Don't give the child anything to drink, although you may use a damp cloth to moisten his or her lips. Keep a close watch on the child's breathing, and if it stops, start mouth-to-mouth resuscitation at once.

Concussion is caused by the brain being shaken or by bleeding within the skull and occurs when a baby or child has suffered a serious bang to the head. The symptoms of concussion may be delayed by up to 24 hours and can be extremely varied.

The baby or child may become unconscious or the signs may be slight. The child may behave slightly oddly, develop an aversion to bright light, have severe headaches or be unusually drowsy. Sometimes the symptoms will include unusual crying, noisy breathing or snoring, vomiting or a discharge from the nose or ear.

If the baby or child has had a bump on the head keep a careful watch for signs of concussion and, if any appear, get emergency help immediately.

Index

Picture Credits

Heather Angel 123 (t, c); **Mark Bolton** 40 (b), 41 (at), 50 (c);
Bubbles Photo Library 59, 118, 121 (t, b), 122, 124;
Bruce Coleman Limited 22 (a), 82 (a), 109 (a), 117; **EMAP Active**
52, 57 (a), 60, 70 (b), 82 (b), 88, 97 (a), 105 (b); **Garden Picture**
Library 6, 9 (b), 10, 12 (b), 14 (l), 15, 16, 17, 18, 19 (a), 20, 22 (b),
23 (a), 24 (b), 27 (r), 30, 31 (a), 32 (b), 35, 40 (a), 43, 44, 47 (b), 49,
53, 54, 64, 65 (r, b), 67, 68, 69, 70 (a), 71 (a, r), 74, 75, 78, 79, 81,
86, 87 (a), 89 (a, b), 90, 91 (r, b),95 (r, b), 97 (b), 99 (a), 100 (br),
106, 112, 114; **John Glover** 9 (l), 19, 23 (b), 32 (l), 34, 96, 99 (b),
108, 116; **Robert Harding** 8, 25, 37, 50 (b), 56, 61, 62, 72, 77, 96 (b),
113, 120; **Jerry Harpur** 29 (a), 58, 105 (a), 115; **Holt Studios** 76,
102; **Andrew Lawson** 42, 66, 85; **Mark Luscombe Whyte** 38;
Clive Nichols 31 (b), 32 (a), 36, 84, 92 (a), 92, 93, 98, 100 (l, tr), 101;
Hugh Palmer 41 (a), 46 (a, b), 47 (a); **Photos Horticultural** 109, 123
(b); **Derek St Romaine** 11 (b), 45, 48 (at, a), 92 (c), 94, 104, 107;
Elizabeth Whiting 11 (r), 12 (a), 13, 14 (r), 23 (r), 24 (a), 26, 27 (a),
28, 29 (b), 33, 50 (r), 51, 57 (r), 80, 83

l:left; r:right; a:above; b:below; t:top; c:centre

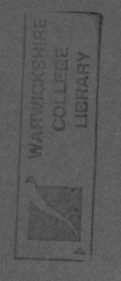